COMMUNE

with the

ANGELS

COMMUNE with the ANGELS

A Heavenly Handbook

Jane M. Howard

A.R.E. Press • Virginia Beach • Virginia

A.R.E. Press
Sixty-Eighth & Atlantic Avenue
P.O. Box 656
Virginia Beach, VA 23451-0656

Library of Congress Cataloging-in-Publication Data
Howard, Jane M., 1951-
    Commune with the angels: a heavenly handbook /Jane M. Howard.
        p.   cm.
    Includes bibliographical references.
    ISBN 0-87604-294-9
    1. Angels.   I. Title.
BL477.H68   1992   92-30231
291.2'15-dc20   CIP

Edgar Cayce Readings © 1971
by Edgar Cayce Foundation
Reprinted by Permission.

I Am the Light affirmation is reprinted by permission (Copyright © 1987 by Consuella C. Newton)
The *Prayer for Peace* was written by John Randolph Price (Copyright © 1984). It first appeared in his book *The Planetary Commission*, which is published by The Quartus Foundation.

Illustrations by Cris Arbo

This book is dedicated to
the Angelic Presence
within each and every one of us.
May the readers of this book
be inspired to unfurl their wings. . .
AND FLY!

J.M.H.

We trust, in plumed procession
For such the angels go
Rank after rank, with even feet
And uniforms of snow.

Emily Dickinson

Contents

Foreword

It is my belief that we are entering a new period of enlightenment on earth in which the mysteries of God are finally being revealed. We are beginning to remember how it was in the beginning, before the fall of humankind.

One of the greatest tragedies of our "fall" into the chaos of misqualified thoughts and feelings is that we created the veil of illusion that has prevented us from being able to consciously commune with the angelic kingdom. With this new awakening, it is now one of our great joys to once again be able to remember these selfless servants of light. Jane Howard's inspiring, timely, and helpful book enhances our memory through tangible experiences and tools that will accelerate our ability to commune again with these angelic presences serving the lifestreams of earth.

Angels are the selfless servants of God; it is both an opportunity and a joy for them to minister to those on earth who seek freedom from their loss of contact with God.

Without fail, the angels answer the prayers and calls of all humanity. They are alerted the instant our hearts stir, when a silent "God help me" arises within our consciousness. At that moment, according to our needs, one or more angels are sent into the fields of our auras to bring grace and assistance.

Angels are God's messengers, yet their service to humanity is not well understood. There is an immutable cosmic law which requires that the call for assistance must come from the octave of consciousness in which the help is needed. Furthermore, the law complies fully with our gift of free will. This means that the angelic kingdom cannot intervene in our lives unless we ask. Once the call for aid has been made, the radiation, presence, and power return on the very current of that plea, according to the requirement of the hour.

The angels abide in the atmosphere of earth. They are ever vigilant in their watch for a flicker of light which signals an "SOS" from humanity to the heavenly realms. The current need is evaluated, then the mission is directed to those angels trained sufficiently to hold within their "feeling worlds" the particular quality of radiation needed to answer the prayer. That quality stimulates a flame of awareness within the heart of the person making the call. As that flame ignites with the requested quality of the angelic host, the person is able to actually magnetize the answer to his/her prayer. And the answer will come, according to our willingness to accept it.

It is by actual experience that the angels grow, develop, and learn the joy that they find within their service. They are even allowed to witness the changes in our consciousness that occur as we are enhanced by their benediction. The happiness and joy that shine in their eyes when they see our transformation is beautiful to behold. They see our stooped forms straighten and our hopeless consciousness fill with faith. They return to the realms of perfection charged with enthusiasm and a burning desire to return earthward, to help again and again, until no lifestream remains which requires any further assistance outside of the flame of divinity blazing in their own hearts.

The truth contained within the pages of this wonderful book will ignite within you a glorious memory of a time long ago when the angels were your loving co-servers. It will also open a door of opportunity that will allow you to renew these blessed friendships. Enjoy!

Welcome home,
Patricia Diane Cota-Robles

Preface

For many years now, I have lived my daily life knowing that an unseen hand is reaching out to guard and protect me. I've felt the energy of an invisible pair of wings envelop me with love when I needed it most. I've personally known, since the age of eleven, that I have a Guardian Angel who is my constant companion.

I have also known for many years that everyone living today has a Guardian Angel, and I know that you have one, too. I believe the reason you are reading this book is because you have been drawn to the angels and want to find out how you can experience them in your life. If you already have had encounters with angels, you may be seeking ways to deepen and expand these experiences, as many others have done.

How do I know there are angels in my life? Because, after years of firsthand experience, I have made them an indispensable part of my life. In my case, I've developed the gift of being able to see and hear them. Unusual, yes, but it's nothing that you can't also train yourself to do.

When I was growing up on a farm in rural Maryland, playmates my age were pretty scarce. So, as a small child, I began to make up imaginary friends. As I grew spiritually, however, this fascination with made-up companions evolved into a friendship with angelic beings who, though invisible to many human eyes, became visible to me during my pre-teen years. My willingness to see the unseen opened the door to the angelic kingdom and filled my life with glorious sights, sounds, wonder, and beauty.

From my Methodist Sunday school and church services, I was taught that I was a child of God. Many children are taught this, but I instinctively *knew* from a very young age that I was loved and protected by God and His heavenly host. I felt that I had a close, intimate relationship with Jesus, too, but I would reach my adult years before fully realizing my connection with God and especially with the angels. It was later still when I understood that many people inwardly hunger to know them as well. Because of this realization, I dedicated my life to teaching others about the angelic kingdom and about God's love for them. I have been communing with the angels ever since—and you can, too.

During the writing of this book, I've found myself reflecting upon the relationship I now have with the angels, and it is difficult to remember when I didn't hear their messages. During my teen-age years, my experiences expanded but were still internal. It wasn't until my late twenties that I was given the inspiration to know what to do with my gift.

My "wake-up call" from God came while I was on vacation in New Jersey. I was shopping at a mall, when I happened upon a "psychic fair." On a whim, I decided to have a numerologist do a reading for me. I paid for a fifteen-minute mini-reading, but up until that moment in my life I had never had any type of psychic or intuitive reading.

The woman talked to me nonstop for one hour. In various ways, she kept repeating the message: "It is no coincidence that you have come for this reading. You are on the verge of a whole new world opening up to you. You are to think carefully about what it is you want to learn; you should also think carefully about what it is you want to *know*. The teachers are ready to appear. The doors are ready to be opened."

The reading turned into one of the most transforming experiences of my life. The reader uncannily told me traits and characteristics that I didn't even know if my mother could have stated as accurately. I remember reflecting on her words and thinking to myself, "What I really want to know is how she did that reading!"

Immediately, I embarked on a course of study that would introduce me to as many spiritual tools as I could get my hands on. I voraciously pursued the study of numerology, palmistry, tarot, I-Ching, and endless others. I dedicated myself to developing my intuitive abilities. The more I learned, the more my curiosity grew to know more about myself and about the mysteries of life. I enrolled in classes offering everything from psychic development and channeling to mediumship. If I thought it could help my spiritual growth, I wanted to be in that class, read that book, or listen to that tape. During this period, I became a Rosicrucianist, a Martinist, and a Mayan, too.

It was also during this time that I joined the Association for Research and Enlightenment, one of the more down-to-earth organizations around, dedicated to the information contained in the remarkable psychic readings of Edgar Cayce. In my spiritual studies, I have found my A.R.E. membership invaluable as it has afforded me accessibility through the mail to the organization's lending library. I have used numerous Cayce readings in researching the topic of angels for lectures and workshops, and have provided in this book some of the best ones.

Whatever subjects I happened upon over the years in my pursuit of knowledge, I found myself always wanting to know more about angels. During the seventies and eighties good material on angels was hard to find. There was nowhere near the abundance of information that's available today. I would ask questions of my many teachers about the angels, but the answers were limited. I decided that I needed to fill this void for myself, and so I embarked upon a quest to uncover as much hidden information on the angels as I could.

Like King Arthur in the movie version of *Camelot*, I "stumbled upon my destiny" when I "stumbled" upon the desire to know more about the angels.

There grew from all my studies, meditation practices, and dedication, a realization that, even though all of us have psychic gifts, mine seemed to be coming more easily to me. I was, in fact, more comfortable in the world of spirit than I was in the physical world. I also began to realize, as I accumulated information on the angels, that I knew more about them than the average spiritual seeker. I was becoming an "authority" on them as a result of my research.

My spiritual path expanded to include the study of healing techniques with teachers from all over the world. Though there were many names and many different ways of healing, I came to realize that there is only one source of healing—God. My dedication to healing expanded into the desire to be of real service to God. When I asked the question, "How can I serve?" the answer came to me in a progression of steps. I gradually began to find my niche as an intuitive reader, massage therapist, and healer. Finally, the three services combined into a technique I called "Transformmassage."

As I began to produce consistently positive results for my clients, I was guided to develop workshops and lectures about the angels. I introduced people to them through individual sessions as well. That is how the Transformmassage technique evolved into the Angelic Attunements, which I describe later in this book. Incidentally, I am also an ordained interfaith minister and member of the Association of Interfaith Ministers. I received my ordination in 1989 from The New Seminary, founded by Rabbi Joseph Gelberman in New York City.

No matter what form my service to the world has taken, I believe this work to be the special way in which God has chosen to work through me. For me, it is God who heals, teaches, lectures, and guides, and I am content to be a faithful servant whose life has been blessed by an intimate relationship with God, Jesus, the Holy Spirit, and the angels.

This book includes many stories of how the angels have touched my life and the lives of those to whom I have lectured and whom I have counseled and taught. I have changed the names of all those whose angel stories I tell, in respect for their privacy, but the stories are all true. The best news of all is how the message seems to be the same in every story—that we are all deeply loved by God and His angels.

To me the stories I share in this book do not merely support angelic theories, but actually demonstrate the truths about the angels upon whom I depend in my life. The angels are the illumined ones and it is they, at God's behest, who light the path of life for us, if we but believe in them and look for the evidence of their guidance in our lives.

When I become anxious, I can feel their love enfold me and reassure me that all is well within my soul. When I experience a physical or emotional challenge, they assist me by strengthening me and giving me courage. All this they will do for you as well. However, when you become aware of them and learn how to commune with them, these blessings will increase for you many times over.

I have written this book as a testimony to the truth that the angels are indeed a reality. Its purpose is to stimulate your awareness of the presence of angels and to open the doors to friendships among all the members of the angelic kingdom and human seekers everywhere.

These constant companions called angels are faithful friends to us, and friendship is built upon mutual understanding. Through understanding, as each learns about the other, friends are able to weave what they hold in common into one energy of love that supports them both.

How do you get to know a friend? There is no better way to understand another than to learn about him or her. In the case of the angels, you can learn about them by reading, by believing, and ultimately by experiencing them yourself through the techniques I offer. By seeking out the angels, one learns how to draw back the veil that separates the kingdom of God and the kingdom of humanity. By making conscious contact with them, you can invite an attunement of vibrations and a blending of energies—a blending of dreams—a blending of vision in your life.

Just as in any friendship, learning more about the other creates more enthusiasm, more love, more of a sense of oneness, and in the process you learn more about yourself. Remember that the angels reflect back to you the message that you are one with all of God's creation, and with faith and patience you will learn that you are one with the angels, too. So as you discover the angels' world of love, blessings, and assistance, you rediscover the world of spirit of which you have always been a part.

I'm especially eager for you to learn more about the angels because I know many people for whom reading about them has triggered their first angelic experiences. It is as if within our beings there are glorious energies that have been stored up and are waiting to be released. The catalyst of activation may be a poem, story, painting, or song. Perhaps your catalyst will be this book.

So come along on this gentle journey into the angelic realm, and think of it as part of an elevator ride in a high-rise building. When you were born, you were on the ground floor. To your perception at that age it was the only floor that existed. You didn't aspire to go higher. Then, through your experiences and learning, your perception of life expanded and you rose to the next higher floor. Those of you who have taken a step to advance your spiritual awareness rose even higher. But when you seek to discover the angels, you will find yourself on the elevator once again as a celestial voice says, "Going up!" There's no limit to how high you can rise into the kingdom of heaven. The angels will help you discover that there are hundreds of floors beyond where you are now. Not only that, but they'll help you discover that you are one with the entire high-rise building and all its occupants combined.

The angels' residence is very special. They live in the perpetual knowledge of God's wisdom and in a profound oneness with God. We humans often forget our divine origin. We experience loneliness, loss, sadness, suffering, and separation. Our celestial brothers and sisters of the angelic kingdom know, however, that there is no separation. Therefore, on our behalf, they perpetually "keep the faith," holding that space for us when we have lost faith in God and lost even the will to live.

I invite you to read this book and walk with me down "Angel Avenue," a pathway that will be paved with the angelic experiences of others and one which, I hope, will lead you to angelic experiences of your own. Each new bit of angelic knowledge that you embrace with your heart is a new brick that you use to help build your spiritual path back to God. Let the angels be your builders.

I hope that through this book you will come to know the angels, learn how to communicate with them, and learn to love them as I do. May their friendship, companionship, and blessings upon your life draw you ever closer to God.

Jane M. Howard
Upperco, Maryland, 1992

✛ ✛ ✛

References to or quotes from the Bible are from the King James Version. The Edgar Cayce psychic readings are identified by a reading number. The original readings are housed at the A.R.E. Library and the Edgar Cayce Foundation in Virginia Beach, Virginia.

Chapter One

Believe in the Angels

" . . . blessed are they that have not seen,
and yet have believed."
John 20:29

No matter how old I grow, my memories will never dim of the joyful childhood I spent on a beautiful farm in rural Maryland. Life on that farm exposed me to the gentle joys of country living and also taught me many important lessons. These lessons helped me to learn at an early age, as the Book of Ecclesiastes reminds us, that for everything there is a season, a time, and a purpose.

Every morning I would awaken to the crow of our rooster and greet a new day filled with exciting experiences. In the evening I'd listen for the crickets talking in the hollow, and I knew that when the guinea hens bedded down in the magnolia tree, it was time to rest. Spring was

1

the time for planting, and fall was the time for harvesting. I learned to appreciate the joy of new beginnings through the birth of farm animals and pets, as well as come to recognize that death is a natural part of life's cycle.

My parents instilled in me a respect for nature and from that respect grew my personal convictions about the importance of cooperation among all God's kingdoms. As I observed my family at work, I learned the importance of stewardship for the earth and the animals in our care. Through my mother's and father's old-fashioned values I learned the message of being responsible for my life and for all that God places in my keeping.

Whether I was romping in meadows full of dandelions or swimming in a clear country pond, all of my farm-life experiences introduced me to the magnificence of God and the awareness that God is glorified in all creation. Even as a child I was able to perceive this. To this day I'm happiest when I can be outside with nature.

I am the youngest in a family of six children. My older siblings all had their lives to live, and since our farm was isolated, there were very few other children my age with whom I could play. As a result, I began to make up friends in the way many children do. Eventually, I became quite comfortable with my "imaginary" friends whom I calmly added to the family circle. All in all, everyone was basically accepting of Janie's "make-believe" friends.

My first experiences with the angels, however, started at the age of eleven when I began to sense the presence of a large being above my bed, watching over me when I went to sleep. The presence was so big that it took on the appearance of a large white canopy of light that enveloped the entire ceiling of my bedroom. In those early years, there was only an awareness between us. I could see the being, and I knew that the being could see me, but neither of us spoke. After a while there was no mistaking that it was an angel, because in my child's perception it began to look just like the angels I had seen on Christmas cards.

I have had a personal relationship with Jesus ever since I was introduced to Him by my family and Sunday school teachers, so I felt a "knowing" within myself that the being in my bedroom was Jesus' friend. I immediately welcomed the angel into my life and never questioned whether or not it was O.K. for it to be there.

As a teen-ager, I became aware of this friend of light being with me at other times of the day, too, and it wasn't long before I began talking to it. Even now, I have a reputation for talking to myself, but I was basically only sharing with my angelic friend what I was feeling and thinking. Through this sharing and the help that I started receiving in return, the angel became my closest confidant.

My sensing of this one angel grew to my realization that there was actually an abundance of angels around and that they want nothing better than to be able to help us all. It was because of this realization that I dedicated my life to teaching others about the angelic kingdom and God's love for them. I have been communing with the angels ever since.

There are many ways to commune with the angels, and I am glad to be able to share them with you in this book. One of the best ways to begin is to allow yourself to experience life's simple joys, like taking the time to appreciate the wonders of nature as I did. I feel as though I was raised by a pair of human angels, Martha and Robert Howard, for that is the gift they gave me as my parental teachers—to take the time to appreciate what God gives us for free.

I believe that the family of God not only includes human beings, animals, and plants, but a vast hierarchy of spiritual intelligences who help govern the universe and help people, like you and me, to keep our mistakes to a minimum. This hierarchy includes the four-and-twenty elders mentioned in the Revelation of St. John and the elemental forces spoken of in the psychic readings of Edgar Cayce. Additionally, there is a colorful, powerful array of beings—angels—whose purpose is to help us live our lives fully and peacefully. God created the kingdom of the angels to assist Him in manifesting the physical form of the nature kingdom and to assist the human kingdom in its growth.

Think of creation as having been released out of a single divine spark. All creation came into manifestation from God—thoughts, feelings, all natural occurrences, all forms, all beings, all life. God not only created the visible but the invisible, and the angels are part of this realm. They were created to radiate to everyone the message of God's absolute good for all creation.

The name "angel" comes from the Latin word *angelus*, which means "messenger." The Hebrew word *malak* used in the Old Testament signifies that angels are "delegates" or "ambassadors" of God. Both terms show that angels fulfill the function of mediating and ministering in the relationship between God and humanity as well as between God and the other kingdoms.

Angels truly are ministering spirits to the human kingdom. *Webster's Dictionary* defines a minister as one who provides aid to another or who provides for their wants or needs. I have personally witnessed the lives of hundreds of clients and students changed by angelic acts of ministration. People have revealed to me stories of the angels coming to their rescue and administering aid in time of need.

Because I so often travel by car, I have had many experiences in which the angels have come to my rescue while I was driving. I recall one of these incidents. Late one night, while coming home from a lecture, I was accelerating to enter the Baltimore beltway from a ramp when the car's gas peddle stuck and I found myself unable to free it. It was a terrifying experience to realize that my car was literally driving itself. I sent a quick SOS prayer right out loud to the angels because I was so scared.

I looked immediately for a clear space on the side of the road where I could pull my car off without hitting anyone. Once I spotted an open length of the shoulder, I threw the transmission into park. The car bounced wildly for a second or two, as it went from fifty miles an hour to a complete stop. After regaining my composure, I attempted to start the car but it wouldn't start. By throwing the gear shift from drive into park, I had probably done some damage to the engine. I prayed to the angels for help because here I was on a major thoroughfare, miles from the nearest exit, and it was ten o'clock at night. My terror of driving a runaway car had subsided, but now I was contending with the fear of being in a disabled car, alone at night. I prayed again to the angels saying, "Please send someone to help me!"

Within minutes, a van pulled up alongside my car with an older couple inside. The first words the woman spoke to me after rolling down her window were, "Don't be frightened. We're Christians." Now I must insert here that many people with whom I have shared this story disagree with my next action because of all the strange things that take place in this world. However, after speaking briefly with the woman, I got into the van and sat beside her. The man and woman then drove me to the closest gas station where I was able to get help.

As we drove, the woman shared with me the reason for their stopping. They had a daughter my age and hoped that by their willingness to help a stranger like me, someone in the future would in turn help their daughter if she found herself in a similar situation. I didn't hesitate to get into the van because of my conviction that the Christ Presence and the angels were with me and, if I were going to die because of this choice, I was going to die a believer. As it turned out, even though I was fifty miles away from home when the incident occurred, the couple lived in a small rural community adjacent to my hometown. They actually knew my family. I truly believe the angels sent those people to my rescue that night.

This is just one of many angel assistances that I have experienced. As a counselor, I am often asked to make contact with angels on behalf of clients, and the unexpected ways in which they help never ceases to amaze me. The fact is that angels can help us today just as they did throughout the times of the Old and New Testaments. Consider some of the profound ways in which they helped the prophets of old and allow yourself to start thinking—right now—about the possibilities of their presence in your own life.

Abraham was visited in his tent by three strangers, one of whom told him that his wife Sarah, at age ninety-nine, would conceive a son. When Isaac was born, Abraham knew that he had been visited by God and His angels. (Genesis 18) Later, when he prepared himself to kill Isaac as a sacrifice, it was an angel who touched his hand and told him that he had proved his love for God. (Genesis 22)

Isaiah saw the glorious angels around the throne of God and heard them chanting, "Holy, holy, holy, is the Lord of hosts: the whole earth is full of his glory." (Isaiah 6:3) And it was a Seraphim who took a burning coal from the altar and touched the lips of Isaiah, blessing him. (Isaiah 6:6-7)

An angel appeared to Zacharias telling him that God had heard his prayer for a child and that his wife Elizabeth would have a son who would be called John. The angel who delivered the message said, "I am Gabriel, that stand in the presence of God; and am sent to speak unto thee, and to show thee these glad tidings." (Luke 1:19) Gabriel was also sent by God to speak to Mary. This appearance is known as the Annunciation because the angel announced to her the forthcoming birth of Jesus. (Luke 1:26-35)

An angel came to Joseph advising him not to be afraid to take Mary as his wife. (Matthew 1:20) Another told him to flee to Egypt, as Herod was trying to find Jesus to kill Him. (Matthew 2:13) The angel would later advise Joseph when it was safe to return home to Nazareth. (Matthew 2:19-20)

When Jesus was thirty years old, He went into the wilderness where He was tested by Satan. Angels ministered to Him there, after He had passed His test. (Matthew 4:1-11) And Jesus Himself taught about the angels. He said, "Suffer little children, and forbid them not, to come unto me: for of such is the kingdom of heaven." (Matthew 19:14) "Take heed that ye despise not one of these little ones; for . . . in heaven their angels do always behold the face of my Father which is in heaven." (Matthew 18:10)

When Jesus prayed in the Garden of Gethsemane, it was an angel who came and gave Him comfort and strength while His disciples slept. (Luke 22:43) On the morning of the resurrection an angel said to the two women who came to the tomb of Jesus, "Fear not ye: for I know that ye seek Jesus, which was crucified. He is not here: for he is risen . . . go quickly, and tell his disciples that he . . . goeth before you into Galilee . . . " (Matthew 28:5-7) An angel freed Peter from prison (Acts 12:11), and St. John in The Revelation described "ten thousand times ten thousand" angels surrounding the throne of God. (Revelation 5:11)

In the Apocryphal book of Tobit, God sent Archangel Raphael to assist Tobias on a journey to collect a debt owed to his blind father Tobit. During the trip a large fish leaped from the water after Tobias. Raphael told Tobias to take the heart, gall, and liver of the fish and make a medicine. When Tobias returned to his home, he was told by Raphael to put the fish medicine on the eyes of his father. At once, Tobit's sight was restored. Later, he heard Raphael proclaim, "I am Raphael, one of the seven holy angels, which present the prayers of the saints, and which go in and out before the glory of the Holy One." (Tobit 5:16, 6:1-8, 11:7-15, 12:15)

There are scores of other angel stories in the Bible—from Lot to Daniel and from Jacob to Elijah—that reveal to us how fully the companionship and guardianship of the angels is given to humankind. Mention of the angels can be found in nearly half of the sixty-six books of the Bible.

These beautiful Biblical stories clearly reveal that the angels have always been "on-call." If they were in a state of readiness then, why shouldn't we believe that they are as ready *now* to help us?

I've seen enough evidence to know that you don't have to be a prophet to receive miracles or messages from the angels. A young woman I know shared with me her personal experience of how an angel saved her life.

This woman works as a nurse in the critical care unit of a hospital. One week, because of illness among the staff, she found herself working double shifts. She explained that when you are on duty at the hospital, adrenaline alone keeps you going, but once you get in your car to go home, exhaustion makes you feel as if your body has run out of steam.

One night, as she drove home after many hours of work, she lost the battle to exhaustion and fell asleep at the wheel. Her car crashed into a utility pole as it drifted off the country road. She was awakened by the impact, only to discover that she was helplessly pinned beneath the steering wheel. In a flurry of emotions, she felt frightened and alone, trapped on a deserted rural road with no other cars in sight. She remembers praying to God for help, when out of nowhere a fair-haired young man appeared who assured her that everything would be all right. She remembers how he moved the wheel with very little effort, freeing her from the wreckage. Moments later, the car caught fire.

The sight of her car on fire was one of the last images she remembered prior to being stirred out of a semi-conscious state by the police. She was still at the scene of the accident, and paramedics were attending to her. When she later asked a policeman the whereabouts of this fair-haired rescuer, the policeman shrugged, saying that no one at the scene fit the description. In fact, the policeman himself was trying to figure out how the woman had gotten herself out of the car, as there was no evidence that anyone had been there at the scene before the police arrived. This woman is convinced it was an angel who responded to her prayers for help.

The angels would also bring us the message of our true identity: that we are one with "all that is," the seen and the unseen, if only we could remember how to hear this truth. They would show us that we are one with the wind, one with the sun, one with the flowers; that we are one with the angels themselves and one with God.

What is the importance of realizing our oneness with God? The answer is simple: it can open our eyes to see and our ears to hear the message of the angels that God is ready to send aid whenever we need it, just as aid was sent to me in my earlier story and to the nurse in the story above.

The more closely we align ourselves to the truth and love of God, the more harmony we will attract in our thinking, our relationships, and our lives. Angels encourage us to be close to God in our vibrations and to strive constantly for a feeling of oneness, the feeling that our hearts are beating in sync with the one heart of the Divine.

When we allow ourselves to feel separate from God, we function under what Alex Jones in his book, *Creative Thought Remedies*, describes as "The Law of Opposites."[1] When we operate under this law, we force ourselves to function amid the simultaneous influences of both harmonious and in-harmonious energies. This creates separation between our personalities and our souls, resulting in our being blind to our affinity with all life—our oneness with the elements, the sun, the flowers, the angels, and God. When we lose this sense of oneness, we trade our focus on truth for that of illusion—the illusion of loneliness, lack, pain, and suffering which can only serve to compound our problems.

By living a life of separateness, we find ourselves preoc-cupied in the world of matter. When this occurs, matter becomes our whole focus in life and we expect it to please us, to entertain us, and sometimes even to save us. Even though the energy that composes matter is eternal, the form of matter is finite and mortal. For this reason, when we rely on that which is finite, we set ourselves up to be disappointed, to feel abandoned and disillusioned.

God has given us the glorious gift of free will, and the angels encourage us to use that free will to choose to attune ourselves to positively charged energy (originating from God), as opposed to negatively charged energy (originat-ing from humans). The angels would encourage us to create light, not shadows, with our lives. They would show us the joy of loving, not hating. They would demonstrate to us the blessedness of peace not war—if we would only look for their inspirational guidance in our lives.

It is a matter of free will to choose to believe or not to believe in the existence of angels. In the words of the Master Jesus, "If thou canst believe, all things are possible . . . " (Mark 9:23) You first have to choose to believe; once you do, you open yourself to unlimited possibilities of contact with the angels, of hearing, seeing, and talking with them.

I believe in the angels because in my own life I have found proof that the angels believe in me. They believe in me just as they believe in you. I vividly remember a cold New Year's Day two years ago, when I suddenly became aware of the presence of my Guardian Angel. As I was in the midst of a divorce, I asked my angel what words of support he could give me for the uncertain year ahead.

I felt directed by my angel to turn on the radio. When I did, I heard a song which up until that moment had been unknown to me. The chorus of the song contained the words, "I am going to be your soul provider." I felt the words touch my heart and give me the reassurance that no matter what was uncertain in my life, I was going to have the support and love of my Guardian Angel. Together, we would be able to face *anything*.

Tears streamed down my face as I listened to the song, and I knew that my angel was conveying the message that I needn't worry about the future, but rather I should find peace in the knowledge that my soul's needs would always be provided for by God. If someone would ask me to think about special moments in my life where I have experienced the power of love, that experience would definitely be included.

Inspired by that "conversation," I asked a typesetter at the advertising agency where I work to typeset a slogan for me. I had it framed and it sits on my desk at home. It reads: "Don't worry about tomorrow. God is already there."

Elaine is another woman who found inspiration and hope from the angels. She is forty-nine years of age and is someone I would describe as "fragile." I feel that this physical frailty is a reflection of the frailty of her emotions. She had come from a dysfunctional home, where she was exposed to physical and sexual abuse. She had undergone three failed marriages, all of which were continuations of her early home experiences. Though childless, she had had two miscarriages during those marriages. In an effort to escape the pain in her life, she became addicted to alcohol. She was in a very despairing state, ill and hurting.

A good friend of Elaine's knew about her troubles. She also knew that Elaine was unwilling to admit her need for help. Not knowing what else to do, this friend gave Elaine a beautiful porcelain Guardian Angel figurine. As Elaine later described it to me, "It was as though that figurine brought a new energy into my life. It became like a 'living' guardian that watched over me."

Whenever Elaine would cast her hopeful gaze upon this figurine, she would unexpectedly receive a loving, warming, encouraging feeling. She credits the gift of the figurine with bringing back into her life the will to live that she had lost. It has to be more than mere coincidence that shortly after the arrival of the figurine, Elaine made the decision to take charge of her life. She joined a support group to help her overcome her addiction, asking the friend who had given her the figurine to be her sponsor.

Of course, the "energy" Elaine felt wasn't from the figurine itself. In meditation I have seen how Elaine was actually helped by two angels—the angelic presence that accompanied the gift of the figurine and the earth angel who gave it to her.

I have seen other startling demonstrations of the protection offered by the angels in my own life and have been told of many such experiences by others.

There was the case of Adam, a young bicyclist from York, Pennsylvania, who was hit from the rear by a drunk driver. The impact from the car threw him from his bike directly onto the path of the car that hit him. Instead of stopping, the car drove right over the top of Adam's legs, but he miraculously escaped with only bruises. There were even tire tracks across his legs. Some time later, Adam allowed himself to be hypnotized to try to understand what happened during the seconds between the impact that threw him off his bike and when the car drove over him— a time span too brief to be recalled by the conscious mind.

The hypnotism revealed that during those few seconds an angelic presence had enveloped Adam in an energy field that protected him from being harmed by the car. He described seeing this presence wrap his physical body in "a cape of neon lights." The electrical force of the angelic presence had transmuted Adam's energy field to a higher frequency so that he came away unscathed from a 2,000-pound car driving over his 165-pound body.

The angels can also enfold us with their messages of love, peace, and joy by actually uplifting our thoughts and inspiring us to greatness. They try to bring into our lives a rich sense of contentment with who we are.

If only we would listen to the beautiful whisperings of the angels who say, "Come, my beloved child of God. Spread your magnificent wings and fly!" then we would begin to truly realize the way of the soul that will lead us to blessings and happiness. Would you listen if you knew you could hear such a message from the angelic realms? There are many ways in which you can do this: by meditating, praying, attuning, and others.

This handbook is meant to help guide your way into an awareness of the world of the angels. If you find yourself feeling confused about your life, where you are going, what you should be doing, who you are, then I suggest that you try using the techniques described in this book to look to heaven and the angels for inspiration. There is abundant help hovering around you and above you every hour, every minute, every second of the day—help that is there for the taking, as Adam and Elaine learned.

With your inner vision focused on heaven and on the angels, you will find the truth of who you are, your purpose in life, and more. It will all come shining through. When you look up to the angels with faith, you can actually see the light of God. You can see darkness dispelled from your life and allow joy to come flooding in. There are many ways to do this.

Always keep your sights set on heaven's laws and try to find heaven's ways in your life. The angels have a loftier perspective on all your problems. By trying to visualize your difficulty from the vantage point of an angel in a cloud of light, you will enable yourself to view the challenge from a broader perspective. God and the angels always see the "bigger picture."

Looking to heaven and God's glorious angels for the reflection of who you are, you will see yourself as one who is unique, special, and loved. Consciously allowing the angels to wrap their wings around you will envelop you with a new peace, a peace from God that can fill you. Just by asking, you can begin to see yourself as God sees you, whole and perfect. You can experience the unequaled satisfaction that comes with this newfound awareness that all is well with your soul and in your life.

No matter how dark you think life may have become, no matter what the problem or dilemma, raise your sights to heaven and look up to God's heavenly host of angels for "enlightenment." Let yourself be filled with the glory and magnificence of heaven. Desire it, allow it—and it will be yours. Let the love of God and the blessings of the angels fill your mind, your body, and your soul. Let healing fill your being. As you read, I want you to be excited about this book, because I am going to share with you meditations and techniques that you can use in every area of your life.

I have been inspired by many authors and poets who have heralded their belief in angels. Flower A. Newhouse, an author of numerous books about the angelic kingdom, wrote, "We are usually eager to expand the circumference of our friendships on the outer plane. Why should we limit our companionships? We should be enthusiastic to widen the scope of our contacts until, through ceaseless searching, our love includes the limitless hosts of all the workers in the service of God."[2]

Charles Fillmore shared his belief when he defined an angel as a "messenger of God; the projection into consciousness of a spiritual idea direct from the Fountainhead, Jehovah. The word of Truth, in which is centered the power of God to overcome all limited beliefs and conditions."[3] When you try the exercises I describe in this book, you will have the opportunity to experience this power that knows no limitation.

Poet R.H. Stoddard wrote of the angels' service in his *Hymn to the Beautiful:*

"Around our pillows golden ladders rise,
And up and down the skies,
With winged sandals shod,
The angels come, and go, the Messengers of God!"

Over and over writers express the belief that angels are messengers of the Creator and are our companions and friends.

When we believe in the angels and learn to work with them, we discover how to bring harmony and balance into our lives and into the world around us. In this way we enable peace, harmony, and joy to exist among all members of God's family. Couldn't your world and the world around you use more peace, harmony, and joy at this time of personal and planetary evolution?

Just as God created angels to be stewards over all nature, He has given each of us a personal angel to be our faithful companion through life. Your angel's role is to assist you while you are here on earth. This angel acts as a messenger of God to guide you, protect you, and love you. Your angel is known as your "guardian" because he or she guards you from harm. Make no mistake. You have a Guardian Angel who loves you as God loves you.

The famous clairvoyant, Edgar Cayce, had a lot to say about guardian angels. According to his biographer, Thomas Sugrue, the discovery of Cayce's gifts while a young teen-ager coincided with an angelic encounter. Cayce, who later became known as "the sleeping prophet," was able to induce in himself a sleep-like state during which he gave psychic "readings" to individuals. In these readings, given over a fifty-year period, he supplied a vast array of information to thousands of people on many subjects. The readings, over 14,000 in all, were assigned numbers to protect the identities of the subjects who went to him.

In psychic reading 405-1, Cayce said, "There are ever, for every soul, those that may be termed the guides or guardian angels that stand before the throne of grace and mercy." Angels are messengers between God and us. They help to make earth feel more like heaven and to fulfill the words of the Lord's Prayer, "Thy will be done, on earth as it is in heaven."

God is the omnipresent source, supply, and support of all creation, and the angels help deliver that supply and support to us. They deliver His guidance, love, wisdom, and good judgment. As God loves us and helps us to develop our talents and capabilities in productive ways, the angels deliver inspiration so we can discover our true gifts. Angels help to manifest God's good for us in marvelous ways and unlimited measure.

It is a wonderful comfort to know that no matter what our age or what we are experiencing in life, God's support is always with us. When life seems darkest, the angels' light can illuminate our path—all we need to do is *believe*.

God has a divine plan for everything. For each of us on the earth He has a plan that encourages us to be all that we can be. He has a plan for every nation and for the earth itself. The angels facilitate these plans for individuals, groups, and the planet, too. Your Guardian Angel will care for you throughout your entire life, offering you assistance as your personal plan unfolds.

In addition to your own Guardian Angel, you also receive—whether you know it or not—the assistance of specialized angels. Just to give you a sampling: there are angels of birth who help mothers and babies; angels who help the soul at the time of transition from the earth plane; angels of healing who work with doctors, nurses, and healers; angels of music who help musicians, composers, and singers; and angels of devotion who are there when people come together to worship and honor God. In fact, there is an unlimited abundance of angels fulfilling God's unlimited abundant plan, amplifying, magnifying, and radiating the ideal of their particular service.

As mentioned earlier, I have heard story after story from people whose lives have been changed by the angels and their message of God's eternal love. One such story is that of Donna who endured a childhood of abuse and neglect. Her mother was a prostitute who abandoned her at two years of age. She never knew who her father was. Her childhood had been a blur of foster homes. Her painful existence continued through relationships that she chose in her adult life. She would become involved with men who were as fearful of an intimate relationship and commitment as she was, so in every one of her relationships the man left. In her mind, this rejection echoed the message that she was unwanted and unloved.

Donna finally came to a point where she felt life was no longer tolerable. She found herself standing on the beach one day contemplating walking into the ocean to end her life. Feeling the intensity of emptiness, she could do no more than fall to her knees and sob hopelessly, calling out to God for help.

When she opened her eyes, she suddenly realized that she had been kneeling in the middle of a large heart-shaped sculpture that someone had carved into the sand. Inside that heart were written the words, "I Love You."

Donna felt something stir within her as she read the words again. She felt as though a tiny light had been rekindled inside her, one that had been extinguished from years of hurt. As a result, she found within herself the courage to seek an ending to the madness she had been living—not through death, but by seeking the help of a counselor.

Donna was blessed that day. She shared this story with me when I met her at one of my workshops. Although she had not seen the hand that inscribed God's valentine in the sand, she believes that the message had been left for her and that she had been guided to the spot by an unseen guardian, an angel watching over her.

Some people feel that belief in the angels is all good and well if you are religiously inclined, but that it is not for everyone. If we believe that God and His creation are for everyone, however, then the angels are for everyone as well. It is a natural and orderly function of the kingdom of the angels to assist all members of the human family, regardless of their race, color, or creed. The angels will assist every one of us in all matters of our lives, whether or not we believe in them. When we do believe, however, they can help even more—and in dramatic ways.

If you still feel uncomfortable with the word *belief* and are struggling with whether or not you should believe in the angels, I ask you to give them, and the ideas in this book, a try. You will be surprised at the difference they can make in your life.

The following little quiz is designed to help you realize how angels have been believing in you and operating all through your life. Take a moment to reflect honestly on your answers. You might be quite amazed at the results.

The Personal Angel Quiz

1.   Have you ever been in a situation in which you would rather have retreated but something gave you the courage to go forward instead?

2.   Have you ever felt like running, but something unexplainable helped you to stand firm?

3.   Have you ever had a gift that you loved but some impulse that you didn't understand encouraged you to give it away? Afterward, did you find yourself impressed by the blessing your gift became for another?

4.   Have you ever known the strong feeling that you had to let go of someone who was close to you, when you would rather have kept that person in your life?

5.   Have you ever been faced with having to take a daring first step, not knowing where you suddenly got the inspiration to do it?

6.   Have you ever been diverted from danger or from making a poor choice, only to find yourself not quite sure who or what protected you?

7.   Have you ever been confused at a critical moment, but received inexplicable clarity just in time?

8.   Have you ever felt that conditions in your life were

so intolerable that you just wanted to cry, and then some funny new perspective suddenly made everything seem so absurd that you began to laugh instead?

9.   Have you ever been amazed as to how a situation that had become a hopeless mess mysteriously turned out perfect for all parties concerned?

10.   Have you ever felt that you were stuck, cramped, limited, or restricted, only to discover, in retrospect, that these blocks were actually gifts that assisted in your metamorphosis and spiritual growth?

If you've answered "Yes" to any of the above questions, it probably means that you've been the recipient of heavenly guidance and, in all likelihood, angelic intervention. It's God's invisible tireless hand that sends the angels to your assistance at these times. The angels see us as "diamonds in the rough" and they are always helping to polish us with God's light.

You may be asking yourself, "All right, if I consider the possibility that angels do exist, how can I experience contact with them?"

I encourage you to open yourself up to the following possibilities: Look for the presence of angels in your life, but not necessarily for a vision. Listen for the angels, but not necessarily for a voice.

In other words, allow the angels to surprise you by communicating with you in the way *they* choose. Your angelic experience may take the form of illumination, a powerful healing current pulsating through your being, or a gentle etheric hug and whisper that tells you that you are loved.

There is a new awareness taking place today about the angelic kingdom as evidenced by the increase of articles and books being written on the subject. There has also been an increase of angel-related merchandise being sold, a whole gamut of items available for angel lovers: angel calendars, greeting cards, guardian angel pins, among others. I'm excited over the fact that the world is becoming angel-conscious because to know the angels is to know God. The angels' whole purpose, after all, is to deliver the light and love of God.

I was recently interviewed by a newspaper reporter about the angels and my work with them. One statement I made in that interview I will share here. "When enough people believe (in angels), when the energy of the angels is moving through enough people, the earth will be transformed to heaven. It will happen in a twinkling."

Many people feel that only gifted ones can communicate directly with or see the angels. This is partly true. I certainly fall into this category, but the gift that I possess is actually given to everyone by God. I hope this book will encourage you to discover your own amazing gifts and develop them so that you can bring angelic encounters into your life, too.

Perhaps I have convinced you to start believing in the potential help of angels in your life. You may be saying, "I'd love to have a relationship with the angels. What must I do?"

Sometimes, all it takes is a bit of sacrifice on your part to get started. Sacrifice is a little word, really, that means making a simple offering. All I'm suggesting is that you consider making an offering to God and to the angels—an offering of good faith. Sacrifice to God your negative thinking, for example, or offer up your self-defeating thoughts and your doubts. There is no reason to take this excess baggage with you on your highway to heaven. All it does is get in the way of real communication with the angels.

In order for you to embrace the understanding of the

angelic kingdom, you must also be willing to offer up—to release from yourself—all the misunderstanding about the heavenly realms that you may have accumulated in your life.

Everyone is invited to dine at the banquet of God. But just as those who prepare for dinner wash their hands first, I encourage you to wash yourself of any negativity that may cast a shadow of doubt upon the angelic experience you are inviting into your life.

Offer up all feelings of self-doubts and unworthiness. Replace the thought, "I am not important enough to have an angelic encounter," with the affirmation, "I AM deserving of the angels. I claim my abundance of their love and assistance." Offer up the feeling of not being good enough and affirm, "I AM a good and perfect child of God."

Before I tell you about the angels themselves and their fascinating realm, I want you to try a simple meditation. Read the description first and then try it from start to finish without the book.

Your "Angelic Minute" Meditation

Begin by closing your eyes and visualizing the light of the angels enfolding you. See yourself sitting quietly in the light from these shining ones. Picture yourself rested and receptive to the sights and sounds of the angels. Believe in their existence, as you visualize them as tall beings of light standing around you. Know that they are there simply because your love and desire has attracted them. You will be truly amazed at the energy you can receive from just this one moment of communing with the angels. Breathe in their light deeply and know that they surround you— because they *do*.

Let the angels clear away the cobwebs of confusion in

your mind. Let them help relax your muscles. Accept from them their gifts of energy, power, love, peace, and joy.

If you are feeling lonely, allow yourself to rest in the light of the angels and feel their closeness. Allow yourself to feel the presence of God with you. It will come as you begin to feel the angels' love and companionship around you.

If something disturbed you today, allow the light of the angels to descend around you and heal the hurt or disappointment. You will be amazed at the change they can make in your attitude. With faith, allow yourself to feel a gentleness and a forgiveness come over you. Harmony will embrace you when you do this.

If there is a future event that you are anxious about, let the light of the angels shine upon you and fill you with God's serenity, calmness, and assurance that your life is always in divine order. Live in the eternal now with that assurance.

The presence of the angels surrounds you and enfolds you in a gentle, protecting mantle of peace.

✤ ✤ ✤

Take a moment every day to experience the angels in the quiet of this brief meditation. Be willing to lighten up your life with the love of the angels in one magical moment of experiencing heaven. It can happen to you as it happened to me. If you take these simple steps and practice often, years from now you will see that desiring to commune with the angels was one of the brightest choices you ever made.

CRIS ARBO

Chapter Two

Learn About the Angels

*" For there is nothing hid, which shall not be manifested;
neither was any thing kept secret,
but that it should come abroad."*
Mark 4:22

We are in the midst of great changes taking place on the earth. One only has to turn on the TV or radio or read the newspaper to become aware of how our world is changing. Tearing down the wall between East and West Berlin and the dismantling of the Communist government in the Soviet Union are only two transformational changes that have recently occurred around us. Because of the magnitude of these changes, many people believe that this is not just another moment in history but a "cosmic moment" that involves not only the human kingdom, but all of God's kingdom.

As individuals, we are becoming aware of our membership in a global family. We now realize that what happens
to our brothers and sisters on the other side of the world
impacts us as well. We are awakening to the truth that we
are all in this world together and that we have come to be
incarnate at this special time to experience individual,
global, and cosmic growth.

This magnificent time of change and development is
actually being experienced by everyone, although at different levels of consciousness and understanding. It is a
time that demands cooperation among all kingdoms, but
at the same time offers an "at-one-ment" between the
angelic host and the human race. Through this "at-one-
ment," those of us who are taking advantage of the opportunities of this "cosmic moment" are learning to work
together hand in hand to bring about the fulfillment of the
words, "Thy kingdom come, thy will be done, as in heaven,
so in earth." (Luke 11:2)

Having personally worked with the angels for years, I've
felt a dramatic increase in their visitations on earth. The angels
are in closer contact with the earth and its people than ever
before. The truth is that we need this help, and it is being
supplied by God through a generous influx of angels.

In the past, it was usually around religious holidays that
the support of the angels was most strongly felt. The reason
was because during these holidays more people allowed
themselves to be aligned with peace, love, and joy—the
keynotes of the angelic realm. At these holiday times the
veil that separated the kingdoms of God and humankind
became more transparent. I believe that the veil has finally
been lifted and that those who choose to walk and talk with
the angels can now do so, just as easily as on any day of the
year.

By engaging in the study of the angelic kingdom, we

allow ourselves to probe more deeply into the mysteries of the Creator. When we enter into the world of the angels, we plunge ourselves into a world of love. Many people feel that angels are merely the fictitious characters of folk tales or images depicted in Renaissance paintings—men and women with wings who fly around doing good. Others don't believe in angels at all because they cannot see or hear them with their ordinary human senses.

The reason for these misunderstandings, of course, is that angels are spirits—they have no bodies. They are made of a finer, lighter material which is not physical in nature. The angels also resonate to a much faster vibration, not at all like the dense vibration in which we operate here in the earth plane. But just because you cannot see the angels doesn't mean they don't exist!

Yet, how is one to picture angels, if they have no bodies? It may help if you think of their vibration as being similar to a spinning ceiling fan. When the fan blades are turning fast, you cannot see them, but that doesn't mean the blades aren't there. The angels vibrate so fast that, like the blades, you can't see them with your physical eyes, but they exist, nevertheless.

We do have other eyes with which we can see the angels. I like to call them the "eyes of the soul." Just as we have ordinary physical senses, we also have superphysical senses; that is, senses whose perceptions are associated with what Carl Jung called the superconscious part of the mind, which is connected to the all-knowing mind of God.

Each physical or outer sense also has an inner counterpart that is in direct contact with God. For example, there is a "soul ear" and a "soul eye." Also, just as each outer sense is in contact with our outer mind, each inner sense is in contact with the all-knowing mind of God.

The words "clairsentience," "clairvoyance," and

"clairaudience" mean "clear sensing," "clear vision," and "clear hearing," respectively. These three kinds of perception refer to the superphysical senses. By consciously developing these inner senses through meditation, prayer, and psychic development exercises, we can become fluent in seeing, hearing, and sensing members of other kingdoms. When we use our superphysical sense of sight to develop our clairvoyancy, we are able to see the angels face to face. The world is full of unseen beings who are waiting for us to explore them with our three additional senses.

Yet angels and humans are quite different in many ways. Angels are pure spirit. The energy that forms their bodies is more subtle than that which forms ours. An angel's entire nature is immortal, whereas we humans consist of an immortal spiritual soul linked to a mortal material body. Angels are not subject to growth and decline; however, as humans, we experience entering a physical body at birth and leaving that body at death.

Angels are God's creations and God's messengers. They possess minds and wills and, in addition, unlimited strength, power, and wisdom. Angels are the stewards of all of God's glorious creation. They govern the lives of animals, plants, flowers, and trees. They also assist in human life and guard the realm of pure ideals as well.

The angelic kingdom is divided into four main categories: angels who work with plant life; angels who work with the elements; angels who work with animals; and angels who work with humans.

The angels who work with plants are known as Devas, and they help govern the life force in the earth's plant life, the flowers and trees. Devas assist with germination and fructification all over the world. A healthy growing plant that we too often assume is the outcome of the sun shining upon a seed planted in the soil is, in fact, the result of the care and nurturing of a Deva. So if you have a prize tomato in your garden, thank your garden Deva!

It is also important to realize that many healers work closely with the Devas. The Devas are wonderful teachers and guides in telling us which plant and flower essences to use in healing. It is also a joyous experience when walking in the woods just to go up and hug a tree! The Deva of the tree will hug you right back!

I remember being enrolled in a drawing class several years ago. The art instructor took the members of the class outdoors to be inspired by nature. Once we were inspired, we were to go back into the classroom and draw whatever inspired us. I found a wonderful tree that I wrapped my arms around and gave a great big hug to. I could feel the Devic energy responding to my hug and returning my greeting with equal love. I was inspired all right, but not to return to class. I played hooky and spent the rest of the day out in the woods.

Elementals, the next category in the angelic kingdom, are literally what their Hebrew name denotes—they are spirits of the elements. The Elementals have "bodies" composed of the elements they govern. You can think of Elementals as meaning "mind of God"—that is: "El" meaning *God*, "e" meaning *of*, and "mental" meaning *mind*. Perhaps you have heard different names from folklore for these little workers, such as sylphs (the Elementals of the air); gnomes, brownies, and pixies (the earth); sprites and undines (water); and salamanders (fire).

Most ancient cultures honored nature in their religions. It is unfortunate that so many of us today have lost touch with the world of nature and have forgotten our kinship with the Devas and the Elementals. But I don't believe that paradise is lost. By loving the earth and sending it our healing energy during meditation, we are giving a message to the Devas and Elementals that we wish to live harmoniously with them and be responsible in our role as stewards.

Members of the angelic kingdom who oversee animals are known as Aqui. Within the order of Aqui are two subdivisions known as Budiels and Folatels. Budiels are angelic beings who watch over the evolution of each animal species. Folatels care for the physical welfare of animals.

The fourth category includes angels who work with humans. It's helpful to remember that all angels are creations of light. When seen in visions or meditations, they usually appear in bright, radiant, stunning, ethereal human form. However, once you have finally seen an angel, you will remember his other distinctly nonhuman expression. Angels have within their consciousness a magnificent "other-worldly" presence. They appear as glowing beings of light with radiating auras that possess such a dynamic energy that they can actually merge with your own energy and give you a light transfusion. It is breathtaking to witness and to feel them merge into your own energy.

While deep in meditation, I have been able to examine the angels closely. I have found that they have force centers and lines of energy within their "bodies of light." They have been depicted in art and literature as having luminous wings of brilliant colors, but the "wings" are not really their mode of transportation. Angels possess the ability to move quickly merely by exercising their wills. The idea of their having wings came about as eyewitnesses throughout the ages described the blur of energy that emanated from their bodies.

One of the best ways to understand how you can experience angels is by examining the fascinating realm in which they exist. On earth you can discover an organized hierarchy of life—from the single-celled protozoa to the complexity of the human being—but in the higher realms this hierarchy continues all the way up to the Source or God. The angelic realm is no different from any portion of God's creation. Angels exist on many levels, and the various classes of angels are charged with specific tasks to be carried out in the universe.

One of the most recognized authorities on the angelic kingdom is Dionysius, who was a contemporary of St. Paul. Mention is made of him in the Bible, in Acts 17:34: "Howbeit certain men clave unto him, and believed: among the which was Dionysius the Areopagite, and a woman named Damaris, and others with them."

After being converted by Paul, Dionysius and his wife Damaris were baptized. A man of prominence, he was taught by Paul for several years and eventually became the Bishop of Athens.

The Golden Legend of Jacobus de Voragine gives the following account: "It is said that Paul made known to him the things that he had seen when he was rapt to the third heaven, and this Dionysius himself seems to insinuate in several places. Hence he has written so aptly and clearly of the hierarchies of the angels, their orders, dispositions, and offices that you would not think that he had learned this of another, but had himself been rapt to the third heaven, and had there viewed all these things."[1]

Manly P. Hall, in his book *The Blessed Angels,* states that Dionysius was present at the death of Mary, the mother of Jesus, and that he was burned as a martyr in 95 A.D.[2] Dionysius is given credit by many of the early church Fathers, including St. John Damascene in his "De Fide Orthodox," for giving an order and system to the hierarchy of the angelic realm which is still highly regarded by many theologians.

In his work *The Mystical Theology and The Celestial Hierarchies,* Dionysius enumerates nine choirs of the angelic

realm in descending order from "Seraphim" to "Angels."
(See Figure 2.1.) He was the first to organize these nine
choirs into three distinct hierarchies, although he con-
fessed to an uncertainty that his interpretation was complete when he wrote, "For the higher we soar in contempla-
tion the more limited become our expressions of that which
is purely intelligible . . . we pass not merely into brevity of
speech, but even into absolute silence, of thoughts as well
as of words . . . We become wholly voiceless, inasmuch as
we are absorbed in Him who is totally ineffable."[3]

The names of the nine angelic orders which Dionysius
refers to can be found in Scripture. In Colossians 1:16, Paul
himself makes reference to some of the orders: "For by him
were all things created, that are in heaven, and that are in
earth, visible and invisible, whether they be thrones, or
dominions, or principalities, or powers: all things were
created by him, and for him . . . "

While all the members of these orders are given the
name "angels," these categories separate them by function
and vibration, depending on their relative closeness to the
throne of God or to the earth. The members of the three
choirs that make up each of the three hierarchies, therefore,
also share in a divine "likeness."

According to Dionysius, the first level of the angelic
realm is known as the "Supreme Hierarchy" or the "Cloud
of Silent Witnesses Before the Throne of God." It includes
the Seraphim, Cherubim, and Thrones.

The name *Seraphim*, translated from the Hebrew, means
"to burn" and, from the Greek, "the inflaming ones." They
are the members of the angelic host who burn with the most
intense energy of divine love. Those who have had visions
of the Seraphim describe them as surrounding the throne
of God and unceasingly chanting, "Holy, holy, holy."

The seraphic host dedicate their invocations to the eternal Creator's glory, and their chanting is a creation in its own right. The energy of the Seraphim sends out a rippling effect throughout God's creation, inspiring anyone who, recognizing the Creator's glory, approaches their lofty vibration.

A musical composer, for example, struggling with a composition at the piano, may connect with that creative energy and receive it in the form of an inspirational series of notes. Within the composer's mind this idea will "burn" with an energy of love that can be expressed in his or her work.

There are many people on the earth at this time who strive to live their lives according to divine love. These persons are attuned to the seraphic vibration. When I am creating something in my life, perhaps when I am "composing" a letter to a friend and want the words to reflect a special message, I invoke the presence of the seraphic host to assist me by inspiring me to write words of love.

The Seraphim are spirits of love. If ever you are feeling unloved in your life, simply ask out loud for the Seraphim to help you. They can dispel any energy that is less than the pure perfection of God's eternal love for you. There is an exuberance about these glorious beings that will envelop you and elevate you and charge you with the essence of love.

While it is the Seraphim who burn with love, it is the Cherubim who emanate the wisdom of God. They assist in intoning the spirit of truth so that every living being is stirred toward renewed growth, rebirth, and evolution. The name *Cherubim* in Hebrew means "splendor of knowledge." The many ways in which the Bible describes their role makes me think of them as "heavenly custodians." It was the Cherubim who were placed in paradise to protect the tree of life. (Genesis 3:24) Moses was directed to make images of Cherubim to serve as guardians for the Tabernacle. (Exodus 25:18-22)

THE
ANGELIC REALM

Throne of God		
HIERARCHIES	*CHOIRS*	*KEY WORDS*
Supreme Hierarchy	Seraphim	Burning with Love
	Cherubim	Keepers of Wisdom
	Thrones	Judgment/Constancy
Middle Hierarchy	Dominions	Administrators of God's Will
	Virtues	Courage/Miracles
	Powers	Law of Cause and Effect
Lower Hierarchy	Principalities	Religions, Nations, Leaders
	Archangels	God's Urgent Emissaries
	Angels	Guardianship/Service
Humankind		

*Figure 2.1: The Three Hierarchies and the
Nine Choirs of Angels According to Dionysius*

The Cherubim are the keepers of wisdom. By invoking them, you are inviting into your life the power of knowing and using the wisdom of God. Whenever something adverse is occurring in my life and I find myself asking, "Why do I need this?" I often ask the Cherubim for insight as to how the knowledge of God is being revealed to me in this situation.

The Thrones work with the glory and equity of God's judgments and are known for their dominant characteristic of steadfastness. They share with the Seraphim and Cherubim the distinction of being closer to God than all the rest of the heavenly host. Dionysius described them as spirit beings who "dwell in fullest power, immovably and perfectly established in the Most High, and receive the Divine Immanence above all passion and matter, and manifest God, being attentively open to divine participations."[4]

When you find in your life that you may be losing faith or trust, invite the presence of the Thrones to radiate their energy of constancy. By their radiation, the Thrones can teach us to use wise judgment in our lives.

To summarize, the first level of the angelic realm, the "Supreme Hierarchy," consists of the Seraphim, Cherubim, and Thrones. The Seraphim inspire us with love, the Cherubim enlighten us with wisdom, while the Thrones teach us to be fair and not to let our feet stray from the path of righteousness.

The second level of the angelic realm is known as the "Middle Hierarchy" or "Advanced Orders." These include the Dominions, Virtues, and Powers and are one step lower than the "Supreme Hierarchy" in terms of their vibration.

Dominions regulate the activities and duties of the angels. They are the administrators of the will of the Thrones who work out God's equity and balance. Dominions are God's "Planning Department," for it is in this realm where plans for the unfoldment of life begin. Dionysius acknowledged the importance of these angels: "They are true lords, perpetually aspiring to true lordship and to the Source of all lordship . . . forever one with the Godlike source of lordship."[5]

When people express to me that there is confusion in their lives as to how conditions are going to unfold, I encourage them to invoke the energy of the Dominions.

There is a saying that encourages us to "Let go and let God" unfold the divine plan in our lives. I believe that God Himself lets go and allows the Dominions to do the administering of His divine plans. The Dominions are the delegators of the angelic host.

The Virtues are the miracle workers. They exemplify the essence of spiritual integrity and are known for making the impossible become possible. Virtues supply miracles daily. If you need a miracle in your life, don't hesitate to invoke the Virtues. According to Dionysius, "the name of holy Virtues signifies a certain powerful and unshakable virility welling forth into all their Godlike energies; not being weak and feeble for any reception of the divine Illuminations granted to it; mounting upwards in fullness of power to an assimilation with God; never falling away from the Divine Life through its own weakness, but ascending unwaveringly to the superessential Virtue which is the source of all virtue."[6]

The essence of the Virtues never falters. I believe that some historical figures such as Joan of Arc, the young French girl who heard voices that inspired her to go out and lead an army, were conversing with the Virtues.

The Powers maintain order on the pathway to heaven. They govern the law of cause and effect. I feel it is the job of the Powers to keep a check on evil entities. They do not use a tyrannical force but rather work with the power of God's light to make dark forces tow the line. If you're feeling overwhelmed by the negativity around you and you're tired from what you perceive to be constant attack, call in the assistance of the Powers. They'll help you to keep the negative influences in check until you are strong enough to hold them back with your own light, strength, and power.

The "Middle Hierarchy," then, consists of the Dominions, who administer the will of God; the Virtues, who are the miracle workers; and the Powers, who keep negative forces in line.

The third level of the angelic realm is known as the "Lower Hierarchy" or the "Ranks of Angels." These are the members of the realm whom we, as humans, come to know most intimately. This third level is comprised of the Principalities, Archangels, and Angels.

Principalities preside over nations, provinces, and rulers. They are the protectors of religions and of world leaders and try to inspire key figures to make right decisions. They neither guard nor direct the policies of a particular nation, because their interest is in humanitarian efforts and the fulfillment of the divine plan for individuals, nations, and the planet. Their duties are described by Dionysius: "The name of the Celestial Principalities signifies their Godlike princeliness and authoritativeness in an Order which is holy and most fitting to the princely Powers, and that they are wholly turned towards the Prince of Princes, and lead others in princely fashion."[7]

Archangels are perhaps the most familiar of all the heavenly host. They have been sent as messengers on missions and in matters of great importance throughout Biblical history. Archangels serve as "interpreters" between the hierarchical members of the higher spiritual orders and humankind. They are leaders who direct legions of angels in the fulfillment of the will of God. Dionysius described them as follows: "The Archangels imprint on all things the Divine Seal whereby the universe is the written word of God; they impart to the soul the spiritual light through which it may learn to read this divine book, and also to know and use rightly its own faculties. The Angels minister to all men and to the things of Nature, purifying and uplifting them."[8]

Proper names have been given to members of Archangels, many of which are familiar: Archangel Michael, whose name comes from the Hebrew meaning "he who is like God"; Archangel Gabriel, whose name means "strength of God"; and Archangel Raphael, whose name means "God heals" or "divine healer." These three Archangels are the only ones mentioned in the Bible proper.

Several other names, however, are mentioned in other ancient literature that was once a part of the Old Testament. During the Nicene Council in 325 A.D., the early church Fathers, for various reasons, eliminated works that had been traditionally included in the Bible. These have become known as the apocryphal books or the Apocrypha. The word *Apocrypha* comes from the Greek word *apokryphos* which means "something hidden." One reason given for the elimination of the books was that their authorship was questioned. (In one of these books, for example, Archangel Uriel, whose name means "fire of God," is introduced to us in the Second Book of Esdras 4:1.)

The third and final choir of the "Lower Hierarchy" of the angelic realm is the Angels. "Angels" is a categorical term applied to the spiritual beings who work most closely with humankind. Their work is specialized and diverse, covering services such as healing, love, inspiration, faith, illumination, justice, and peace—to name just a few of their innumerable ministries.

Angels work in specific areas to fulfill God's plan. For example, Angels of Transition and Angels of Birth would be listed under the broad category of "Angels" in the heavenly telephone directory. There are also Angels of Art, Angels of Music, and Angels of Poetry. There are Angels of Worship and Angels of Healing and, of course, Guardian Angels. Guardian Angels are God's gift to us at the time of our birth. These holy angels escort us on our journey through life. They protect us, defend us, guide us, and minister to our needs.

By their vibration and the duties they fulfill, Angels are closer to humankind than any other celestial spirit. All angelic members can be invoked by human beings, but it is from the choir of Angels that the Guardian Angels come forth, because they are the closest in vibration to the earth.

One of Cayce's readings shares insights into the roles of Angels and Archangels: "With the bringing into creation the manifested forms, there came that which has been, is, and ever will be, the spirit realm and its attributes—designated as angels and archangels. They are the spiritual manifestations in the spirit world of those attributes that the developing forces accredit to the One Source . . . " (5749-3) Thus, Angels are manifestations of the attributes of God.

While there are a multitude of Angels performing services for the human kingdom at this time, some perform specialties that make God's higher energies more accessible to us on earth. These include the Angels of Spiritual Fire, Solar Angels, and the Angels of Karma.

Angels of Spiritual Fire work directly with individuals who wish to use the spiritual flames. These are nonphysical flames, comprising the colors that correspond to the twelve rays (see Figure 2.2)—which can be visualized in meditation and used to transmute negative energy. (One of these, the violet fire, will be discussed in Chapter Seven.)

Solar Angels "step down" the vibration of the frequencies of God's solar perfection so that we on earth can receive it. Because of their focus, we are able to use these frequencies to picture perfect health, eternal youth, radiant beauty, abundance—every aspect of God's perfection for us. Solar Angels help us make our lives an expression of God's perfect thoughts for us.

The Angels of Karma work with individuals and the great process of evolution. They help us to master our thoughts, feelings, words, and deeds so that we learn and evolve from our experiences. They help us to understand that we are responsible for our actions and that life is a school room intended for us to learn. Their service is always that of divine love. Whereas the Powers govern the law of cause and effect, the Angels of Karma work directly with humans to help them understand the law as it operates in their individual lives.

To summarize, the third level of the angelic realm is comprised of the Principalities, who watch over religions, countries, and their leaders; the Archangels, who are our important emissaries; and Angels, who specialize in particular services and provide us with our Guardian Angels.

In exploring the lofty realm of the angels, we have covered the wide range of their vibrations and functions, from the Seraphim down to the Angels. Dionysius' writings have served as our model, used for centuries to help those who want to know more about how Heaven is organized. In teaching you about the angels, however, I now want to expand your understanding and help you further as you continue reading this book.

In addition to the ninefold nature of the angelic realm, Tellis S. Papastavro's *The Gnosis and The Law* makes reference to what is called the twelvefold nature, or the twelve virtues and nature, of God.[9]

When God created the universe, His divine mental action radiated twelve rays of light, each representing one aspect of His twelvefold nature. Each ray or pure concept goes forth from God's mind eternally and crystallizes one of His virtues. You can think of God as a giant sun, with His light shining through the prism of consciousness, dividing itself into twelve distinct rays. Each ray conducts the essence of its pure ideal into every aspect or level of consciousness in the universe. (See Figure 2.2.)

Patricia Diane Cota-Robles, in her book *Your Time Is at Hand*, identifies twelve Archangels and their feminine counterparts called Archaii, who participate in the manifestation of this twelvefold aspect of God. Individuals can attune themselves to the ideal of each ray *and* enlist the aid of each ray's Archangel and Archaii to manifest that ideal in their lives. According to Cota-Robles, these rays make up what she calls the "twelve Solar Aspects of Diety."[10]

People often ask me at my workshops about the twelve rays because many are only aware of seven rays and seven Archangels, but unaware that the number is actually twelve. The aspects of God have always totaled twelve, but for millennia humanity has been only operating with the lower seven aspects of God's great gifts. Along with the other dramatic world changes I mentioned at the beginning of this chapter, great spiritual changes are occurring as well. One of the most important of these is that our consciousness is rising from the limitations of the third dimension to a new awareness of fourth-dimensional activities, such as the angelic realm. As the earth and humanity ascend into this higher realm of consciousness and vibration, it is easier for us to perceive our Higher Selves which are united with God at the superconscious level. This is because of the renewed influx of the last five rays.

THE TWELVE RAYS OF GOD'S CONSCIOUSNESS[11]

Ray	Key Words	Color	Archangel and Archaii	Divine Attributes	Seed Thought
1	God's Will	Sapphire Blue	Michael/Faith	Faith, Power, Protection, and Order	Energy-Light
2	Enlightenment	Yellow	Jophiel/Constance	God-Illumination, Wisdom, and Understanding	"As Above, So Below"
3	Divine Love	Pink	Chamuel/Charity	Divine Love, Adoration, and Tolerance	Divine Love
4	Purity	White	Gabriel/Hope	Purity, Hope, Resurrection, and Ascension	Vibration
5	Truth and Healing	Emerald Green	Raphael/Mother Mary	Healing, Concentration, and Inner Vision	Cycles
6	Ministering Grace	Ruby	Uriel/Donna Grace	Ministration, Selfless Service, and Grace	Law of Cause and Effect

7	Freedom	Violet	Zadkiel/ Holy Amethyst	Forgiveness, Mercy, and Compassion	Transmutation
8	Clarity	Aqua-marine	Aquariel/ Clarity	Perception, Discernment, and Clarity	Polarities
9	Harmony	Magenta	Anthriel/ Harmony	Balance, Harmony, and Assurance	Harmony
10	Peace	Gold	Valeoel/Peace	Peace, Comfort, Inner Calm, and Balance	Balance
11	Divine Purpose	Peach	Perpetiel/Joy	Victory, Fulfillment, Joy, and Purpose	Perfection
12	Transformation	Opal	Omniel/ Opalescence	Transformation, Transfiguration, and Rebirth	Oneness

Figure 2.2 Communing with the angels can be enhanced by meditating on the divine ideals of the twelve rays.

Humanity was originally designed to manifest all twelve energies in a similar way to God. The angels are today encouraging us to respond once again to the inner call to be the glorious twelvefold light beings that we were in the beginning. In other words, they ask us to awaken to our true identity: a beloved child of God who is composed of all twelve aspects of the God Presence.

The Archangels and Archaii are beloved brothers and sisters from the celestial realm whose assistance is helping us evolve beyond the limits of our finite minds. Invoke them into your life and they will selflessly respond. As we expand our awareness of the twelve rays, they will guide us in learning how to use these twelve qualities of God perfection in our lives.

The chart shown in Figure 2.2 is a tangible tool to use in your daily meditation work. It can assist you in reaching your full potential, merging with the God Presence. Read the chart over completely. Then quiet yourself and ask the angels to reveal to you which ray you should concentrate on first. Your angel will guide you as to which one will be of most help to you at this time in your life. You can close your eyes and let your finger run over the chart. Stop where it feels "right." Or just wait for a "feeling" to come to you as you read through them. It might take several tries before the "message" gets through, but don't give up. Your angel won't.

Focus on the names of the Archangel and Archaii for that particular ray. Invite these angels into your life. When you have a special health need, you seek out a specialist, so think of the Archangels and Archaii of each ray as specialists in helping you understand the energy of that ray. Concentrate on the key word, as you visualize the color of the ray surrounding you. See yourself being filled with the color. See the color being magnetized to you and also radiating from you. Read the divine attributes of the ray and think about ways in which you can apply them. Come up with one practical action that you can do today that will exemplify that quality. Now read the seed thought associated with the ray. You can use these seed thoughts as subjects for powerful meditations at any time. The seed thoughts can lead you even deeper into the higher realms of God's truth and manifest even further the essence of each ideal.

Work with a particular ray until you feel a sense of completion. Then at that time, ask the angels to reveal the next ray with which you should work. Allow yourself to experience all twelve rays—you can spend a week or a lifetime on this, but it's well worth it.

An important question that I'm often asked during my lectures and workshops is, "What about Lucifer and the fallen angels?" Though I am one who does not like to give energy to the dark forces in my lectures or my writings, nevertheless, I feel I should mention them here. Besides the angels who make up the nine choirs of the angelic realm, there are fallen angels, who fell from grace with God. These are the angels who, led by Lucifer, rebelled against God's laws. Before we were created, Archangel Lucifer governed the kingdom of the angels and was known as the ruling prince. Like all angels, he was originally created as an angel of light to glorify and serve God. The following describes his power: "Thou art the anointed cherub that covereth; and I have set thee so: thou wast upon the holy mountain of God; thou hast walked up and down in the midst of the stones of fire. Thou wast perfect in thy ways from the day that thou wast created, till iniquity was found in thee." (Ezekiel 28:14-15) What was that iniquity? It was pride and covetousness. Lucifer wanted to be the ruler over heaven and over all of God's creation. He wanted to be worshiped, not to worship God.

As a result of his desire to replace God, there was a rebellion in heaven between the angels who were faithful to God, led by Archangel Michael, and the angels who allied with Lucifer. Defeated by Michael, Lucifer and his followers were banished from heaven and have struggled for control on the earth ever since.

Even though I acknowledge the existence of Lucifer and the dark forces, I choose to follow the example of Jesus, as described in Luke 4:8, when He said to the tempter, "Get thee behind me, Satan." The truth I live by is that God is the one omnipotent force in the universe and that the temptings of the dark forces are merely more opportunities for me to see God's magnificent light when contrasted with that darkness. How often in our lives have we "seen the light" when conditions had become dark and dismal? That is a sublime contrast indeed.

One Cayce reading expounds upon this concept: "It has been understood by most of those who have attained to a consciousness of the various presentations of good and evil in manifested forms, as we have indicated, that the prince of this world, Satan, Lucifer, the devil—as a soul—made those necessities, as it were, of the consciousness in materiality; that man might—or that the soul might—become aware of its separation from the God-force." (262-89)

I believe that while there is a fallen angel named Satan, I simply choose not to believe *in* him. I believe in God the Father, Christ the Son, the Holy Spirit, and the angels whose service glorifies the Trinity. Even though ours is a world filled with the influences of the dark forces that at times appear to be causing great chaos, I believe that God will have the last word—and His last word will be good; furthermore, it will be broadcast joyously by every member of the angelic realm.

Once you understand the services of the angels who reflect God's glory and goodness, you can attune your consciousness to that group of angels and allow their special quality to radiate to you and manifest in your life. As the venerable gospel hymn states, "Abide with me." You can actually invite the specific angelic essence you desire to abide with you, and in the next two chapters I'll show you how.

·CRIS ARBO·

Chapter Three

Meditate with the Angels

"Finally, brethren, whatsoever things are true,
whatsoever things are honest, whatsoever things are just,
whatsoever things are pure, whatsoever things are
lovely, whatsoever things are of good report; if there be
any virtue, and if there be any praise, think on these
things."
Philippians 4:8

The purpose of this book, as I've stated before, is to show you how to commune with one of the most beautiful, wise, and loving parts of God's creation—the angels—and this chapter describes one way of doing this.

God created the angelic kingdom partly to express His external desire to answer our calls for help and partly to answer questions when we are in need of enlightenment. Angels are always on call, and meditation is one of the best ways by which we can commune with them. Through meditation we can actually "call up" the angels. Their number is listed and it's not a costly exchange. It's free and accessible to all, twenty-four hours a day.

What is meditation? It is our inner mechanism for receiving the sights and sounds of heaven, and for remembering who we really are. It is the focusing of the mind on the subtler energies of the inner universe. It is our opportunity to expand our consciousness and to connect with the realization of the divine truth that we are actually one with God. With practice, meditation can be a transformational and transcendent experience.

The discipline of meditation became widespread in the U.S. in the 1960s, but it has been practiced for thousands of years worldwide—from Judaism to Christianity, from Hinduism to Buddhism. However, there is much about meditation that is still misunderstood, especially here in the West. Many people make it more complicated than it needs to be, and others make it too simplistic. Joel Goldsmith, in *The Art of Meditation,* explains it this way: "As we begin to recognize our good as the gift of God, we let the reasoning, thinking, planning mind relax. We listen for the still small voice, ever watchful for . . . the Father within. It will never leave us nor forsake us. It is our permanent dispensation. This listening is the art of meditation, in the learning of which we come to a place of transition where truth leaves the mind and enters the heart."[1]

Meditation with the angels is an invitation for them to speak to us and to make themselves known to us. It is not an attempt to reach the angels, because they are already with us. In meditation we achieve a state where our energies blend with the energies of the angels so that an awareness of them and their love permeates our being.

Silence is the key to meditating with the angelic kingdom. It is necessary because it allows us to quiet our conscious "thinking" mind, so we can experience the angels as they commune with us and attempt to introduce us to the wonders of the spiritual world.

Meditation takes practice and patience. As a result of your commitment, though, you can experience a powerful communion with the angels. It can bring you the health benefits of increased vigor and reduced stress. A sense of tranquillity can be yours as the angels come to you and fill you with their love and healing. The experience of meditating with the angels can leave you with a longing for the opportunity to experience this wonderful bliss again and again. The time you spend in prayer and thinking about the angels is the groundwork that can open the door for powerful angelic meditations.

There are many ways to attain a meditative state with the angels. The main item to remember is that you should practice at the same time each day so that a rhythm is established in your life. This will produce the best results. I meditate with the angels twice each day, once in the morning upon arising and once in the evening just before I go to bed.

I make my meditation time a ritual of joy. When I begin, I invoke the angels enthusiastically into my ritual. "Invoke" means to welcome and invite them to be a part of my meditation, a part of my day, a part of my life. My invocation can be a simple "Good morning, sweet angels! I welcome you into my life" or "I love you, angels!"

Angels are important members of your spiritual family. If this is your first "conversation" with them, formally invite them to join you. A simple invitation from your heart will do, such as "Come share this moment with me." Say it right out loud, and don't think it's childish. By your invitation, you are stating your intent and desire to communicate. You can add real power to your invocation by saying in a loud clear voice: "In the name of the Father-Mother God, I ask the Thrones to gather around me and help me as I pray."

Invocations can be either a gentle welcome or a powerful call for assistance. Try the following the next time you seek protection:

"Archangel Michael, protect me here and now from danger and attack! Raise me into your mighty protection, enfold me with your strength, and stand guard around me! With your shining, glorious sword that tamed the dragon, keep all harm from me!"

As you ready yourself to meditate with the angels, wear loose comfortable clothing so you feel unrestricted. If this is your inaugural experience with meditation, try to find a quiet, undisturbed place in your home where you can meditate every time. You may want to burn incense, arrange flowers, or light candles. You may want to add the ambiance of relaxing music.

As you make yourself comfortable, begin to relax into the space you have created for yourself. The position of the body isn't important—you may use a chair, sit on the floor, or lie down. Your body knows instinctively how to relax so just follow your body's suggestion.

Arrange your position so that no bright light is falling directly on your eyes. Relax and breathe deeply for a few seconds. Free yourself from all the chores you need to do during the day and from all that you may have done just prior to this meditation time.

Approach your meditation with the intention of expressing your love to the angels and communing with their love for you. It's better not to enter this state expecting results, because you'll be telling your mind in advance what it's going to see. According to *The Secret of the Golden Flower*, a respected ancient Oriental text on the subject of meditation, "The decision must be carried out with a collected heart, and not seeking success; success will then come of itself."[2]

Next, I always like to begin with prayer. I think beforehand about the words I will say to the angels. I use this time to make requests for healing for myself, my family, and friends. I also pray for anyone with whom I feel I am not in harmony—people I may be having difficulty loving. By doing this, I release myself from conflict so that I can make room for the messages and experiences I am going to receive.

After praying, I allow myself to focus upon an aspect of the angels. For example, I may think of the word "peace." In my years of meditating with the angels, I have come to know that their peace is a very calming influence in my life. So when I think of their peace, I find myself becoming that peace. To bring this about, I think about peace and ways in which peace can be expressed. I "breathe in" peace for myself and exhale peace to the world. I begin feeling utterly at peace and in tune with the angels. I like to sit quietly and continue to "breathe in" their peace and power. Then, I'll take a few moments and just bask in the radiance of their love and light.

In my classes on angelic awareness people ask me how to trust what they see and hear during their meditations. That brings us to the important subject of imagination. There is nothing that is not imagination, for all that exists sprung from the imagination of God. Imagination is a natural part of the outer mind, the source of all ideas. It is always there and you can always tap into it. Even those who think they don't have any imagination or who complain that they have trouble visualizing can develop a vivid use of imagination through practice.

It always amuses me that the same people who tell me they have no imagination are the ones who are able to vividly visualize the worst that could possibly happen to them. That's their imagination working overtime—just not in a way that supports their highest good.

So in your meditations with the angels, I encourage you to "make things up." Go ahead and imagine the best for yourself. Your imagination is a powerful gift which your mind shares with the mind of God. By intentionally using it, especially at the beginning of learning to meditate, you lubricate your powers of visualization for deeper meditation later.

Through imagination I have reached higher realms in my meditations where I tap into ideas that are beyond my knowledge and experience. I have tapped into the all-knowing Mind and have been blessed with the uncanny ability to witness some of the loftiest places of heaven. The root word of *imagination* is the Latin *imago* or image. By using your imagination you tap into the image of God that is within us all. To use your imagination is to make use of divinity in your life. A proper name for imagination is God. To work with your imagination in your daily meditations is to work with God.

If you practice meditating with the angels regularly, you will eventually feel a shift giving you the sensation that your room is full of light—as if you, too, were a part of the heavenly host. You may also specifically feel the presence of your Guardian Angel. You may feel a warmth around your body, a presence around your shoulder, or a movement of energy like a "breeze" of light.

When I'm sitting with the angels, if I sense a sign or message coming to me, I accept it. It could manifest as a visualization forming in my mind's eye or a gentle inner voice talking to me. If there are no messages, I thank the angels anyway because I know my day will be filled with their blessings since I at least remembered to invite them into my day.

I find that often what happens during meditation is not as important as what happens afterward. The benefits will eventually manifest in your daily life. You will find that the love you experience in meditating with the angels will remain with you all through the day. This spiritual experience can give you strength to handle whatever problems you face in the material world.

As you practice meditating with the angels, you will begin to see a gradual development of the ease in which you are able to quiet yourself, to "go into the silence," and to feel the presence of the angels. With regular practice, it will be easier for you to go into a meditative state and quiet yourself on demand.

The following meditation ideas have been designed to put you in touch with your Guardian Angel. By using them regularly, you can increase your ability to commune with the angelic kingdom. Allow yourself to focus daily on your heartfelt desire to commune with your own Guardian Angel and you will see results.

Guardian Angel Meditation

Begin by thinking of the color you will use by which to identify your Guardian Angel. Whatever color comes to mind, trust that it is the one to use. In a future meditation, you may receive the thought to change to a different color.

For now, visualize that color as a small pinpoint of light within your heart. Let the pinpoint of light grow increasingly larger until it fills your heart, your chest, and continues to expand until it fills your whole being. Imagine or visualize that you *are* this color, from the top of your head out to the tips of your fingers and down to your toes. Pretend that the angels have taken a paint brush and painted you inside and out with this color.

By allowing yourself to "feel" the expansion of this color as it grows larger and larger, you are opening yourself to receive the love that your Guardian Angel feels for you. Let the color move through your pores and fill the room with its essence. Then, visualize it as it fills your house. Let it expand farther, filling your community, your city, state, country, the world, and the entire universe. By expanding the color in this way through visualization, you are actually sharing your Guardian Angel's love with all of God's creation. Adding your love to it will enhance the experience. Your meditation should be not only an experience of love for you but for the universe as well.

After you have experienced your Guardian Angel as a simple color, focus your receptivity and try to sense your Guardian Angel's gender. Even though angels are neither masculine nor feminine, they can manifest as representing either the masculine or feminine nature of God. To assist us, our Guardian Angels take on the guise of one gender or another, depending upon what support is needed in our lives. So, sense within yourself whether your angel is masculine or feminine. You may want to make these statements to yourself and see which one rings true for you: "My angel is masculine." "My angel is feminine."

Once you have ascertained the gender of your Guardian Angel, allow yourself to sense his or her presence with you. It's all right to sense your angel as energy. If you don't actually see a form in your imagination—a face, shoulders, and "wings"—be satisfied with the feeling alone, and try to hold on to that presence with love and gratitude.

Now ask yourself for a name that you would like to give as a gift to your Guardian Angel. Listen for the prompting from your inner voice and trust the response. It may be a name that you loved as a child. If the angel's gender is the same as your own, it may be a name you wished you had been called. It may be a Biblical name or a formation of vowel sounds that you find appealing. Let yourself be open to the experience of naming your Guardian Angel.

Next, decide what it is that you want to discuss in your meditation with your angel. Take a look at your life and think about your concerns. Your angel is your best friend. So what would you like to receive from your friend today? It can be anything from asking advice on how to handle job stress to how to attract more abundance into your life. You may want help in developing your psychic abilities or knowing what steps you can take to expand your spiritual awareness.

Once you know what you desire, talk to your angel about what is going on in your life in that particular area, whether it be relationships, finances, spiritual growth, or health concerns. Share the whole scenario with your angel. Explain what's going on from the way you see it. Share your thoughts, feelings, and emotions. Go ahead! Speak out loud or share it silently by thought.

Be honest and straightforward. "Over the past month, I've been feeling more and more overwhelmed. I feel as if I'm not in the driver's seat of my life anymore, as if I'm losing control. There seem to be so many demands on my life. I'm always feeling anxious, as if there's not enough time to do all that needs to be done. I feel that my meals are just a blur. I want to slow down, but I just don't know where to start. It all seems 'bigger' than I—the demands of my job and home. I just want something to grasp onto. Please show me how I can take control of my life again."

When you feel that you have fully explained what is transpiring in your life, visualize yourself standing before a field. Now visualize a path taking form before you. This is the path that is going to lead you to an answer. Allow yourself to follow this lovely green path as it leads you to a place of harmony which I call "Harmony Hill." Know that your Guardian Angel walks with you to this hill. Feel the peace and love that surrounds you. Stop and relax at the top of the hill. Feel yourself sitting on the hill in the middle of this lush landscape, surrounded by bright radiant colors and joyful birds. Watch. Listen. Feel. Make everything clear in your mind. Stay as long as you like and be nurtured by this place. Take in all the scenery around you as the experience charges you and expands you.

If at any time during your meditation there are outside distractions, simply let your Guardian Angel brush down your aura to soothe and relax you back into your meditation and your place of harmony.

Now in your mind's eye see a bridge appear before you—a bridge of light. Get up and walk across this bridge that leads you into the angelic realm. Don't be just a spectator and see yourself walking across the bridge— actually *feel* and *imagine* it as you get up and walk. Focus your awareness on walking across the bridge and, if you need to, say to yourself, "I am walking across the bridge with my Guardian Angel." Once on the other side of the bridge acknowledge that you have crossed over into the angelic realm.

You have crossed this bridge in order to ascend into a higher level of consciousness. Once the bridge has been crossed, there are an unlimited number of places you can visit. Ask your angel to take you to a library where you can look up information that will help you with your problem. Feel yourself enter a great white building and choose a room. Enter the room and see the stacks of thick, old books. Take one of the heavy, ancient books from the shelf and open it. Read the words or symbols that are shown to you.

Instead of a library, you may ask to be taken to a teacher who will shed insight on what you need to know. Ask the teacher for an answer. Know that you are opening yourself up to answers and experiences from many sources in the angelic realm. You can attend classes with other seekers. You can enter great halls of wisdom. You can ask someone to recite a poem to you or sing you a song. Let your Guardian Angel guide you to the new information you are seeking.

If at any time you are shown something you do not understand, ask that it be presented in another way. Do not limit yourself on your journey. If you need clarification, ask for it and trust that it will be given. You may ask to be taken to a healing garden, where an Angel of Healing awaits you. Call upon this angel, then listen to what that angel has to say. Reflect on and accept what is given to you in your journey. Again, know that you may ask questions at any time. Visualize not only your own Guardian Angel, but other angels walking before, behind, and below you. Let this angelic "fortification" help you inwardly feel the support of the angels as it radiates healing and strength to you during your meditation.

Be active in your meditation. Build a bridge, walk down a path, select a site that you want to visit. As in all areas of your life, be responsible in your meditation. Make it happen!

When it is time to bring your meditation to a close, thank your Guardian Angel for being your guide, and offer the angel a blessing. Give thanks for the experience that you had during this meditation and for the information you received or anticipate receiving as a result of this experience of crossing over into a higher dimension.

✛ ✛ ✛

The purpose of seeking to commune with the angels is not to escape, not to get out of your mind or out of your body. It is rather to be who you are in the body you live in and also to experience yourself as you really exist in a higher transcendent realm, the angelic realm. By meditating with the angels, you will enrich your daily life by truly bringing some of the energy of heaven into earthly consciousness. You will experience a higher vibration of wisdom and faith, courage and love.

In meditation we learn to cooperate and communicate with the angels. The angels have an abundance of God's knowledge and understanding which they want to share with us. We need to be willing, however, to be active, alert, and awake as we meditate with the angels.

When we "call up" the angels in meditation, we are connecting the telephone lines of our earthly exchange with those of the angelic realm. We are tapping into heaven's wisdom, love, and strength. We are asking the angels to share with us all the treasures that are stored for us in heaven. Through their messages in meditation, the angels can actually become a source of guidance, courage, steadfastness, inspiration, and love.

Some of you may hesitate to open up the lines of communication with the angels because you are afraid of dialing a wrong number and finding yourself talking with a negative or dark energy. I cannot emphasize enough that where your intent is, your mind will follow. If you are seeking to communicate with the blessed angels of light and thus invoke these angels to participate with you in meditation, know that you are attuning yourself only to their vibrations. There is no reason to be afraid.

Where meditation is concerned, I am one who has diligently worked at it. I believe that when we are encouraged by the Bible to "tithe," that is, to give one-tenth of our abundance to God, it also means to give one-tenth of our day. Since a day is 24 hours, I strive to give 2.4 hours back to God in prayer time, meditation time, and time spent serving others. I make every effort to keep the times I designate for meditation every morning and evening. Because of my commitment, I have evolved to a point where I am able to communicate with the angels even when I am not in a contemplative, meditative state. You can do this, too, or at least come close by practicing diligently.

My experiences in meditation have been many. I have heard quiet whisperings of messages. I have seen light shows of colorful energies. In one particular experience I was feeling very frustrated about not knowing how to combine my services as a massage practitioner and as an intuitive reader. I had attended a massage school and had received my American Massage Therapy Association membership. I had developed my psychic abilities to the point where I was very fluent in giving messages. I didn't know which of these talents I should be developing into service to others, and I was feeling pulled in two directions.

I went into meditation, but I must confess that I was very rude in the way I demanded an answer to my problem. I said, "I want to talk to God directly—no one else but God!" I went into the stillness and immediately was given the vision of my being picked up by a very large hand and being placed in an even larger high chair. I heard a voice question me, "Now what is so important?"

I replied, "I need to know what I'm supposed to be doing. Am I to be doing massage or should I be doing intuitive readings?"

The voice replied, "Yes to both your questions. You are to be doing both."

I was then shown an image of Michelangelo's painting "Creation of Man," in which God's finger nearly touches the finger of Adam. I was given the message that I would be "touching" those whom I serve with my hands through giving them a physical and energetic massage and at the same time touching them mentally with my words through a psychic reading. I saw large-sized letters move across my mind's screen with the word: TRANSFORMMASSAGE. I was told the name of the technique would be "Transformmassage" and that people who experienced it would have the opportunity to be transformed on a physical, emotional, mental, and spiritual level. At the conclusion of the vision, my consciousness was brought back to the room.

After that experience, I took action and promoted the technique of Transformmassage. I worked with clients for several years until the time when I was directed to turn my energies toward working with the angelic kingdom and Angelic Attunements. The Transformmassage technique has been a very important part of my evolvement to where I now work directly with the angels in my service. It gave me a wonderful experience of working with all levels of the body simultaneously, which is an important part of the Angelic Attunement technique I will be describing in a later chapter.

I have also had humorous messages given to me in meditation. In one particular session I was expressing my stress over having to pay attention to what appeared to be an overwhelming amount of detail work in my job. I was questioning why I had to do so much. The angels gave me the vision of a bed. On the bed was a large donkey. I saw a bedspread drift down from heaven and cover up the donkey. I intuitively knew the angels were saying that the detail work was important in order to keep my "donkey" or "ass" covered! From that meditation I gained respect for the importance of attention to details.

Meditation has provided great solace to me when I have had to confront the reality of loved ones making their transition. In one such instance, I was experiencing tremendous fear over the possible loss of someone I loved very much. I had gone into meditation and immediately had a sensing that even though physically I was sitting in a chair, my body was being turned in a horizontal position. I was taking on the shape of a boat and began floating in space.

As I looked up from my horizontal position, I saw an image of a very frightening figure which I recognized immediately as having a "Grim Reaper" persona. This being did everything he could think of to scare me. I suddenly realized that I wasn't frightened by him or his actions at all. I told him I wasn't afraid of him and looked him right in the eyes. His scary image was then transformed into a beautiful being of light who was sending vibrations of love to me. He said, "I know you aren't afraid of death and that is why it is part of your service to comfort others who may be afraid."

Still in the form of a boat, I floated to a beautiful crystal mountain. As I approached the mountain, the center of it opened to me so that I could pass through it. As I went into the center of the mountain, I saw an image of what I believed symbolized leaving this world at the time of transition. I floated through a tunnel and there were light beings all around me. I could feel the light and the peacefulness that people who have had near-death experiences describe. I remained floating in that peaceful state until the closure of my meditation. From that experience in meditation, I received assurance that no matter what happens, I will have the courage and faith to face it and to be a source of comfort, strength, and inspiration to anyone who is facing this transition.

I would like to share another powerful meditation experience I had with the angels. In early 1989, I had been receiving messages from the angels that I would somehow be involved in a community service organization and that the angels would be involved as well. In fact, I had been told in meditation that they would be assisting those who got involved in this service to the point that it would appear as if the angels had come to earth. I was quite anxious to determine what the service would be, but my mind was a blank.

Several months later I found myself in the throes of separation from my husband of eighteen years. It was a very painful transition. Even though I was finding it extremely difficult to move forward with my life, I never stopped counting my blessings every day—and I had so many blessings. True, I was no longer married and wasn't sure where my home would be as a result of the marital property dissolvement, but I knew how much love and support I had from my family, friends, employer, and co-workers—even my pets. Many people gave me support during this time of transition and change. I thanked the angels every day for the blessings in my life. But even with these blessings and the life-saving contact with the angels through those difficult months, the pain and fear were formidable. I needed a way out, a way to express and to heal what I was feeling. I still didn't know what the angels had meant by "community service."

Then one day during meditation I heard a gentle voice say, "You are blessed to be a blessing." In my visualization I suddenly saw the following word spelled out in huge Ben-Hur style lettering: W I N G S. All I could think of was the wings of a bird, but I simply couldn't figure out the significance.

The voice then spoke to me again and said that the letters stood for "Women In Need of Guidance about Separation." It was to be an organization that would give women who are going through such a transition their "wings" to fly above the pain and sadness, and I was to be its founder. It is now a self-sustaining nonprofit organization which provides one-on-one support for women. A woman counselor "angel," who has successfully made the transition through separation and divorce, is assigned to help a woman who is in the midst of it. I have since witnessed many times how beautiful friendships have evolved among the women involved and how they have truly found their "wings."

Through my meditations I have been advised that these human "angels," in fact, bear the blessing and assistance of a heavenly realm angel, as they administer caring and compassion to their assignees. This organization, which I was led by the angels to establish, was the mechanism by which I was able to heal myself of the trauma of divorce. I owe this assistance directly to my communing with the angels.

Your own Guardian Angel may also lead you through experiences in meditation that will give you a sense of knowing what is right for you to do and not do. You will find that regular meditation can help you develop a sense of trust in God and the angels. If you are sincerely seeking to find truth for yourself, to be one with God, to live a life of love and compassion, the angels will assist you in bringing into your life, in both the physical and spiritual realms, people who reflect those attributes.

God gives you the gift of each day to shape your destiny—a day filled with opportunities called "moments." You can fill those moments with anything you wish. I encourage you to begin each day by spending some time with the angels in meditation. If you do, you will be beginning your day with moments of peace, love, and joy. Pour out your heart to the angels in the first moments of waking. Share your problems with them and ask for their divine guidance in resolving them. Thank God for all the blessings in your life and bless the angels for all the wonderful services they perform for you.

After years of meditating with the angels, I have found that the communication I experience through communing with them extends beyond the few moments I spend in the morning. You, too, can discover that your morning meditation with them prepares you for your day in the same way. Just as an orchestra tunes up before a performance, your meditation time will allow you to attune your body, mind, and spirit so that throughout the day you will be able to converse and commune with the angels at will. As you make time for the angels on a regular basis, you will find that communication with them will extend into every moment of your life, if that's what you desire. The ritual of meditation can lead to spontaneous and continuous communication and support from the angelic realm.

I would like to introduce you to a powerful meditation concerning the Archangels and Archaii of the Twelvefold Aspect of Deity discussed in Chapter Two. Remember that the twelve rays or qualities of light emanating from God to all life are amplified upon earth through the assistance of the Archangels and Archaii. By invoking their help in our lives through prayer or meditation, we can be lifted in consciousness and find relief from our own self-created illusion of separation. We can truly learn from the Archangels and Archaii how to realize our unity with God.

As we seek this gentle instruction by holding the qualities and virtues of God in our consciousness and letting these qualities radiate from us into the world, we will magnetize and draw to ourselves even greater energy from the cosmic realms. As a result, this will increase our ability to radiate energy farther out and to touch the lives of those around us.

It is the commitment of the twelve Archangels and Archaii to assist our evolvement on the earth, until all life has ascended and is spiritually free. The more we invite the Archangels and Archaii and the twelve rays into our lives, the more we will draw their radiation to us and the higher our own vibratory rate will become. We will begin to recognize that heaven and earth are truly one. Ask these beloved brothers and sisters of the celestial realm to assist you in fulfilling your divine plan. They will joyously and selflessly respond. These divine light beings are co-workers in our individual, group, and cosmic missions of spiritual growth and transformation. They will only work toward our highest good, and their assistance will sustain us beyond the comprehension of our own finite minds.

By daily experimenting with this meditation practice, you can become proficient at maintaining a force field around you that is charged with the qualities and virtues of God. I suggest that each morning you refer to the list of key words in Figure 2.2, and select one that will benefit you, your friends, loved ones, co-workers, and whoever else for whom you may wish to pray. After you have selected a quality, proceed with this meditation that invokes the Archangel and Archaii of that ray.

Archangel Meditation

Seated in an armless chair, allow yourself to feel relaxed and at peace. Visualize the sun in your mind's eye, as you invoke the presence of the Archangel and Archaii. Call for the virtue or quality you wish to radiate by saying aloud:

In the Holy Name of God "I AM," I invoke now the Archangel _____ and Archaii _____ to guide, guard, direct, and empower the Divine Plan on earth through me today. CHARGE me with the quality of _____ from the heavenly realm. In the Sacred Name of God "I AM," I now expand and project this glorious God energy of _____ into my own body, mind, and spirit. I project it into humanity and all life to further God's plan on earth. I give my own blessing that this radiation of energy through me shall accelerate all life forward now toward the Divine Plan fulfilled. I AM grateful to Archangel _____ and Archaii _____ and all the angelic host for assisting me in this meditation. I love you and thank you for your love.

Now breathe in the light of the sun, raising your arms up from your sides until they form the walls of a cup. Forming this cup symbolizes the offering of your body, mind, and spirit to be filled with the light of the virtue you selected. Breathe this ray into your heart. Hold your breath to the count of four. Exhale to the count of four, lowering your arms as you exhale. Feel the ray of light going through every pore of your skin. Rest to the count of four. Repeat this exercise twelve times. At the conclusion of the twelfth exhalation, rest peacefully and allow yourself to experience any messages, blessings, or visions that you may "imagine."

✦ ✦ ✦

It may take practice—memorizing the invocation will help—but as you learn this meditation without having to look at this book, your visualization and experience can be that much more full and exciting. I suggest trying this meditation every morning for a month. Then, note any difference in the way you feel. See if you notice how much more the angels manifest in your life.

There are several interesting ways in which you can enhance your experience of communing with the angels. One important way is to create an altar. In my home I have set aside a special location that is solely dedicated to God. It is where I worship God in my home and where I do my prayer, healing, and meditation work.

An altar can be any type of structure—a nightstand, a TV table, a coffee table, or whatever you wish to use. I have chosen to use an antique hope chest given to me by my mother. The altar can be located in any room you wish, but it should be permanent and the space kept free from all other activity. You will need to make the space sacred in your mind and heart and make sure everyone else in your household understands and honors this.

On my altar I display photographs of people in my life whom I love and who love me. I also have photographs of my beloved pets. I keep fresh flowers on the altar during the spring and summer, and I also place crystals and stones there which have special meaning to me. I place inspirational books on my altar from which I read during my prayer time.

On my birthday and at Christmas, when people give me

gifts, I place them on my altar prior to using them so I can give blessings back to the person who gave the gifts to me. People often give me photographs of others who are in need of God's healing, and I place these on my altar. This altar is a place of power in my home. The picture of the object of one's prayers is the best form of visualization.

From years of having worked at my altar, a vortex of energy has gradually built up around this sacred space. Creating this field of light requires no particular technique. All it takes is regular daily prayer. The light field gathers there through the momentum of my own prayers and from the energy radiated from the angels who come there to work with me.

In teaching people about the angels, I often encourage them to go to churches, temples, or mosques so they may connect with the energies that have been built around those areas. A magnificent example of this effect is the vortex of energy around the altar of the National Cathedral in Washington, D.C. Because of the glorious services that have taken place there, a vortex has been built from the sincere and faithful hearts who have worshiped God there and also from the blessings that have been showered over the altar from the angelic realm. These energies have been particularly enhanced by Angels of Devotion and Worship. Such "showerings" are not limited to the altars in houses of organized religions, but can occur anywhere a faithful heart regularly prays. An altar in your home will also be blessed by the angels, for as you honor God you will be honored.

As mentioned earlier, on my altar I also keep certain crystals and stones. I would like to teach you how to create and use your own cherubic crystal, because of the energy it can add to your meditations and prayers.

As I shared in Chapter Two, Cherubim in Hebrew

means "knowledge of God." In one reading Cayce honors the cherubs by saying, "About the entity's whole experience there are cherubs, that are more in keeping with the thoughts—or that are an influence for good ... Hold fast to those experiences and expressions that may bring to thee that activity of thy guardian forces unfolding before thee ... " (2520-1) You can "Hold fast to those experiences" by holding a properly prepared cherubic crystal during your meditation.

A cherubic crystal is one that you have activated in meditation and which has been charged by the Cherubim. You need to obtain a clear quartz crystal. Follow your inner promptings as to the appropriate size or shape for you. Once you have selected the crystal, hold it between the palms of your hands. Ask out loud for the wisdom vibration emanated by the Cherubim to flow through you and into your hands so that the stone will become charged with the Cherubim's vibration. Prepare the crystal once in this manner and you will never have to do it again, unless someone tampers with it or changes its programming.

When I sit holding my crystal, after I've prepared myself to enter meditation, my hands can feel it becoming warm as it is being charged and blessed by these wonderful beings who encircle the throne of God. When you look at your crystal, love it for it, too, possesses an angelic intelligence—that of an Elemental. Know that your clear quartz crystal is now a symbol of the clear consciousness you will be aspiring to when you come to your altar to meditate with the angels. While doing this, know that you are a giver and receiver of the love that is amplified by the crystal.

As you learn more about the angels and practice meditating with them regularly, you may wish to use a number of activated crystals to work with the different choirs of the angelic realm. For example, you may have a crystal which you have charged with the energy of the courageous, miracle-working Virtues, another for working with the Thrones, and so on. But remember that you don't *have* to have a crystal to commune with the angels, only that it can help.

Make time for a regular meditation with the angels. In order to help you, here's a handy list of five easy steps to follow:

Be AVAILABLE—choose a time and a place where you won't be disturbed. Create an altar and use a crystal if you wish. Make yourself available to the angels by bringing yourself into a meditative state.

Be ASSERTIVE—maintain your focus on your meditative experience; when your thoughts wander, bring them back lovingly to your purpose.

Be ALIGNED—align yourself to the angels through opening your meditation with prayer and invocations. Use visualizations in which you contemplate the qualities of God radiated by the angels.

Be APPRECIATIVE—thank the angels for the insights and love that they share with you during the meditation and throughout your day.

Be ACTIVE—the angels may call you to action by moving you to do something, as I was moved to be the founder of WINGS. Follow through on the messages you receive. It adds an important sense of completion to your meditation.

The benefits and blessings will come through for you if you simply try to use regular meditation as a method to commune with the angels. What can enhance your meditations even more? Asking the angels to assist you in your prayers—which is the subject of the next chapter.

·CRIS ARBO·

Chapter Four

Pray with the Angels

*"Thinkest thou that I cannot now pray to my Father,
and he shall presently give me more than
twelve legions of angels?"*
Matthew 26:53

What is the difference between praying with the angels and meditating with them? Essentially, prayer is conversation with the heavenly beings, whereas meditation is an attempt to hear their answer.

A Cayce reading describes meditation as *"emptying* self of all that hinders the creative forces from rising along the natural channels of the physical man . . . "* (281-13) In other words, we are making room in our own personal temples for the energy we will receive during the meditative experience. Words are not necessary for one to succeed in meditation, but they are the hand tools of prayer—whether spoken or unspoken.

Prayer is a spiritual conversation with God. It's a way of communicating with God in which you send your message outward rather than receive one inward. When you pray, you affirm your birthright as a son or daughter of God to make personal requests, petitions, and proclamations to the Creator.

In order for prayer to work we must first believe in the power of God to make changes in our lives. The principle is similar to when a child is learning to ride a bicycle. The child must first admit a degree of faith in the idea of bicycling. So it is with prayer. With faith, you can let go of what is troubling you and turn it all over to God, acknowledging that God has the power to give you answers and guidance.

There is power in prayer because, through your words, you are invoking the one presence and the one energy behind all life. God's sustaining presence and power are ready to help in any situation in life, and the angels encourage us to ask God daily for what we need. In their book *Prayer Can Change Your Life*, authors Dr. William R. Parker and Elaine St. Johns write, "The measure of the help you can get through prayer is limited only by the size of the cup you hold up to be filled."[1] God is unlimited in what He can do.

When we pray, we remind ourselves that God is a part of our lives and that wonderful things can happen just for the asking. I marvel at the many ways in which God has brought good into my life because of my prayers.

Prayer is really a survival technique for me, and my work with the angels has intensified my belief in its importance. I pray upon waking up in the morning and in the evening before I fall asleep. I really enjoy it, because my connection with the angels has shown me that it's just one more way in which I can commune with them. I pray with others in church services and in prayer circles. I pray at various times throughout my work day, for myself and for others. During my angel workshops, I invite people to give me names and blessings for which I can pray. That's how much I enjoy seeing this powerful tool work in our lives. Prayer is so important to me that I often wonder why anyone tries to survive without it.

I always use an invocation at the beginning of my workshops to acknowledge the sacredness and ceremonial energy of the cooperation between the earthly and heavenly kingdoms. The invocation is really a prayer offered to the angelic realm. I pray to the angels for their guidance and assistance in revealing to the workshop participants the love and light of God and the angels. The invocation invites the angels to join us and makes known our sincere desire to welcome them into the workshop and into our lives. I recommend that you try to recite an invocation before you pray, in honor of the divinity within you and of all the angels who are about to join you in prayer.

When you want to pray there is no need for a special setting. You can use certain words and mantras, if you like, but it's not necessary. You don't have to induce an altered state of consciousness either, as you do for meditation. There should be a naturalness and spontaneity about communication through prayer. You should just allow it to flow from you, regardless of the state you are in when you decide to pray.

Of course, people pray all the time without any particular awareness of the angels. However, this chapter is intended to share with you a powerful secret about the role angels can play in your prayers. The fact is that when you team up with the angels they add tremendous strength to your prayers. The idea is to allow yourself to become partners in prayer with them.

When you pray with the angels, you can create a celestial sanctuary wherever you are. By invoking them to pray with you, you are actually joined in your sanctuary by members of the angelic host. The angels recognize the holiness of prayer and are always willing and waiting to join you. All you have to do is ask them.

When you invoke the angels to pray with you, you call them forth from the angelic realm to hear your request. Your invocation can be as simple as, "In God's name, I invoke the angels to add their power to my prayers." Another example is the following invocation which I have written on your behalf—a prayer for everyone who reads this book:

"O Father of Light and Mother of Love, I invoke the glorious angels into the lives of my readers! I call forth the Seraphic and Cherubic angels, the Archangels and all members of the angelic kingdom to surround those who are reading this book so they may feel the charging radiation of the angels in body, mind, and spirit.

"May this book open a door for each and every reader, offering the opportunity to believe in the angels sincerely, accept the angels openly, know the angels personally, live and experience the angels daily, and be angelic eternally. I send my gratitude and love to all of the blessed angels, and accept my call as being fulfilled in God's Most Holy Name . . . I AM."

Angels are actually "living prayers." Through their service to humanity they *become* the energy of prayer in action and expression. They love nothing better than to join in your thanksgiving to God, to rejoice with you in the blessings in your life, and to be a part of your worship and adoration of God.

The angels are ministering spirits who want to amplify, magnetize, and multiply your prayer requests to God. Even a few moments of prayer, spoken in the knowledge that they have surrounded you, can uplift you. As the angels commune with you—wherever you are—they can help renew you in your "energetic" prayer sanctuary.

Many people have misconceptions about prayer that originated in their childhood when they were taught to think of God as being somewhere "out there" or "up in the sky." God is often erroneously depicted as a kind of judge who will either reward or punish us on some divine whim. As a child, I thought of God as a huge being with a long beard who was very stern and always looking down from behind the clouds checking on what I was doing. Such notions create the illusion that God is outside of us and that through prayer we are begging and pleading for what we need in our lives, only to be given it or denied it by this controlling external force.

I have a favorite way of imagining how creation took place. It's as though God struck a single note, and that note or vibration was love. Now, that original note vibrates eternally through all life; it resounds in everything and reverberates in all directions. No matter where it travels or how far it goes, it is still the same note; it is still love. Love is the inner reality of God's infinite creation. God is love.

Since all creation came from love and is love eternally, God is in all creation. God is in me and in you. I am that never-ending note, and so are you. You are made of eternal love, and so am I. We are children of God, forever one with His power. In reality, there is no separation from God because we are a part of that same note. I, therefore, believe that it is our divine right to have health, freedom, peace, and prosperity. When you need help to achieve something in life, you can go directly to God through prayer.

The angels are always waiting to assist you in discovering for yourself that you are love. They are always waiting to hold a prayer meeting with you. They will assist you in your blessed moments of prayer, so that you can easily make contact with "Prayer Central"—that love essence or note of God that resonates right within the center of your heart.

Prayer is a holy and empowering experience as it acquaints you with the presence of God in your life rather than the absence of God.

Prayer is an activity of creation. The Seraphim and Cherubim that encircle the throne of God are said in Scripture to chant "Holy, holy, holy" unceasingly with adoration and love for God. It is believed that the chanting of these words maintains a creation energy that filters through the angelic realm and finds its way to humanity where it can be felt as support, blessings, and inspiration. By their existence, these blessed angelic beings are chanting a prayer that is a song of creation. When you pray, your prayer, too, is a song of creation, and the same creation energy then becomes active in your life. When you pause to pray, you become like the Seraphim and Cherubim. You encircle the throne of God with the heart and energy of your prayers.

Because of the many misconceptions about God, I have found in my work that people often find it difficult to have faith in their ability to communicate with God. For this reason I encourage people to begin reaching out to God by praying first with the angels. Others may feel overwhelmed as they contemplate the intense concept and energy of the Creator, so I encourage them to get to know the angels, God's messengers, first. Just as in some families it is easier for people to speak with a brother or sister about their needs rather than to go directly to Mom or Dad, I encourage people to pray with their celestial siblings, the angels, and know that God hears their prayers.

Helen Steiner Rice poetically described our uncertainty about praying in "God, Are You There?"

"I'm way down here,
"You're way up there . . .
Are you sure you can hear
my faint, faltering prayer."[2]

So if you are someone who is concerned about God hearing your prayer "down here," trust in the angels' messenger service for a quick delivery of your prayer to God. It may help to consider how angels take the role of mediator, much like the ancient practice of sending a letter of introduction with a messenger. The angels are God's messengers of introduction, introducing you to His love, illumination, peace, and harmony. I am fully aware that when I pray to the angels for help, the answers and energy I receive through them originate with God. All good gifts come from God; however, the angels were created to be God's assistants in creation—but I put them on overtime! I find comfort in praying with them because it is my belief that God created them to pray with me and to amplify and magnify my prayers.

How does one go about praying with the angels? To begin, let your prayers reflect your personality. In other words, start by being yourself. You can pray inwardly, silently, or aloud in various ways. While you can speak your prayers at will whenever you wish, there are two special forms of verbal prayer that you should know about.

The first is called a "decree." A decree is a simple declaration—it doesn't ask; it commands. With a decree, we use words to command the Source of all creation to take an active role in manifesting what we need. The truth of the power of decrees is stated in Job 22:28, "Thou shalt also decree a thing, and it shall be established unto thee ... "

The key energy behind a decree is the force of the "charged" declaration we make. The power in our command sends forth an energy that establishes in the universe our demand for the fulfillment of that for which we are decreeing. As an example of a decree, you may give commands such as the following. Stand and assertively state to the angels:

"Charge, charge, charge me with the strength of Archangel Michael, so I shall not lose my faith!"

"Expand, expand, expand in me the healing light of Archangel Raphael so I am bathed in healing light throughout the day."

You can create your own decrees and use them for particular requests and special occasions. They are a powerful way to manifest good in your life or in the lives of others.

The second form of verbal prayer is an "affirmation." Affirmations are positive assertions of truths that we want to manifest in our lives. They can be used effectively to counter the influence of negative statements that sometimes creep into our thinking.

Many people I know are inclined toward negative thinking. They have been taught to think life-negating thoughts from a very early age. Some people allow past mistakes, remembrances of injustices, vain regrets, or the loss of friends to fill their thinking. It is worthwhile to follow the advice given to Lot by the angels, "Escape for thy life; look not behind thee ... " (Genesis 19:17) Many people continually look behind them and are consumed by regrets from their past.

An affirmation is a mini-prayer that disciplines the mind

into thinking more positive thoughts. When I make an affirmation, I am speaking a positive truth about something I want to experience in my life. In so doing, I draw upon the power of the spoken word. The Bible shares with us the message of the power of words in John 1:1 with the statement, "In the beginning was the Word, and the Word was with God, and the Word was God." It is my belief that the "Word" described here refers to the sum total of God's creative power, that same creative energy that goes forth with every word we utter as well.

Charles Fillmore in his book *The Revealing Word* maintains that the act of affirming allows one to "hold steadfast in mind or to speak aloud a statement of Truth . . . that asserts confidently and persistently the Truth of Being in the face of all appearances to the contrary."[3]

An affirmation is usually phrased in a way that means something to us personally, such as:

"I see myself as I truly am: successful, radiant, and endowed with the potential to achieve."

"I am patient, for I know that a pattern of good is unfolding."

Using affirmations effectively requires more than just the verbal repetition of phrases. When you say your affirmations, think about the words until they reveal clearly in your mind the ideas contained in them. Use your imagination as you speak your affirmations. Picture the new patterns of thought within you. As you see in your "mind's eye" the new you living a new life, the words you are affirming will impart strong messages to your subconscious mind.

When Moses was speaking to the burning bush, God said that His name should be known as: "I AM THAT I AM." (Exodus 3:14) The words "I AM" reflect the oneness of all life (perceiving itself as "I"). When you say the words, "I AM," you are invoking the creative power of God to fulfill whatever follows those two words. It is an invocation to God to manifest what you say. For this reason it is important to pay attention to what statements you are making when you use these words. Have you ever said, "I am sick and tired . . . " or "I am so lonely"? By making negative statements such as these you are actually drawing to yourself the energy of that which you want to eliminate.

Planting positive thoughts in your mind is somewhat like planting a garden. The ground really does not care what is put into it. It will grow whatever is planted. Your subconscious mind also does not care what it is fed. It will give back to your outer world whatever you have put into it. Don't expect a rose garden to be blooming in your life when you are letting the brambles of negative thoughts grow wild in your mind. Fill your mind with positive thoughts and affirmations and you will see your world move from negative to positive experiences.

There is one particular form of affirmation that I would like to mention, and that is a "vow." A vow is defined as a solemn affirmation, a promise, a pledge. It is an oath that you make directly to God; hence, it is the most sacred affirmation that you can make. Making a vow is quite a serious business.

When I found myself going through the transition of marital separation, one of the questions that haunted me was, "What happened to the vow I had made to God when I got married?" I realized that the marriage had ended, but what happened to the energy of my oath before God? I sought out many friends for their answers, but none of their words satisfied me and the question persisted, "What happened to the vow?"

One day in meditation, the angels provided me with a

most unexpected healing by revealing to me that even though my marriage promise made to another human being had ended, my vow to God remained intact. My pledge "for better or for worse" was a commitment to God to gratefully experience all the lessons of my marital life. But in a deeper sense I was still married to God through my vow, and our love for each other would be eternal.

These two forms of verbal prayer, decrees and affirmations, are examples of the power contained in the spoken word. When we verbalize such statements we send forth this energy from within our beings, transporting the thought that we wish to manifest in our lives. What happens when we do this is that the spoken words accumulate energy and help us magnetize the fulfillment of our goals. The words become "God in action."

When we use positive affirmations and decrees, we are making a dynamic request to the universal life force to bring good into our lives. Think about what it is you want in your life and apply the principles of using affirmations and decrees daily. Affirm to the angels all the good that you want to experience in your life.

Because of my own personal belief in the importance of positive, affirmative prayers to the angels, I have created a set of cards each of which contains an affirmation associated with a particular angelic intelligence. I use these cards in my workshops by inviting participants to draw one and receive an angelic blessing through the message on it. Such messages include: The Angel of Change—"I AM making positive changes in my life"; The Angel of Honesty—"I AM honest and direct about what I want and don't want in my life"; The Angel of Intuition—"I AM recognizing my intuitive ability."

You do not need these cards to begin reprogramming your thinking through positive verbal prayers. You can create your own cards with your own messages. One way to use them is to keep one with you as the focus for that day, week, or month. Remember that reprogramming is what we are doing to our minds when we use affirmations; we are changing the channels on our ruts of habitual thinking. You can use affirmations from great spiritual teachers or make your own list. If in the past you affirmed your lack of money, love, peace, or happiness in your life—then simply change the channel and affirm abundance and prosperity.

Your prayers, then, can be silent or spoken aloud in the form of decrees or affirmations, or they can be chanted or sung. Many don't realize, however, that nonverbal expressions such as dance, art, or writing can be used as prayer, too.

You may choose to pray with the angels through a spiritual prayer journal or you may address your prayer letters to the angels in a diary. I prefer a diary. I find that I can keep a running account of my daily prayers that way. I simply start by writing at the top of the page, "Dear Angels—" Then I proceed with sharing my hopes, dreams, fears, anxieties, and my wants and needs. I use my own words, and my prayers are private among myself, the angels, and God.

Your prayer journal will provide you with opportunities for healing through the disciplined act of writing and letting your feelings have a place of expression. Your words become your written prayer. When you take the time to commune with the angels through written prayer, you give yourself permission to share with other members of God's creation what's going on in your life. It's a written acknowledgment that you are important in God's divine plan for earth and that God is important to you. You are saying to yourself, by the action of keeping a journal, "My thoughts, my desires, and my needs are deserving of space on this page and of space in God's universe." Of course, you can pray verbally with the angels anytime and anywhere. You can say a long or a short prayer. It can be a plea in the form of "Help me, angels" or a brief *alleluia* of "Thank you, angels!"

One morning, as I was driving my car, I began to approach an intersection between the main road I was driving on and a side street. I received a warning from my Guardian Angel who said, "Look at the line of cars waiting to pull out from the side street." He showed me that the person in the first car was feeling very frustrated over not being able find a break in traffic.

Now you need to understand that this came in a flash. One moment the thought wasn't there, the next moment it was vivid in my mind. With my thoughts focused on everything I had to get done that day, I ignored the warning.

Just as I got to the intersection, the driver pulled her car in front of mine and then, realizing that she couldn't make it, stopped right in the path of my car. I hit the brakes and prayed, "Help me, angels. I'm going to collide." I felt the brakes grab and the car slow down and I watched, as if in slow motion, as I came closer and closer to impact. Just inches from the woman's car door I came to a stop! As I sat there overwhelmed by the possibility of what could have happened, I looked up to heaven and said out loud, "Thank you, angels!"

I feel it is very important to have an "attitude of gratitude" in your life. When you are thankful, the angels respond by giving you more blessings for which to be thankful. Prayer isn't just for when things go wrong. Use prayer to praise God and the angels for all they've done for you in your life. God was greatly pleased by that one particular shepherd who sang praises to him. The shepherd, of course, was David and the Psalms are his songs of praise—his songs of creation. To this day David's prayers create inspiration and strength for anyone who reads them. Creation energy is eternal.

The only real requirement for praying with the angels is that you believe that your prayers will be answered. You can even give a "thank you" at the end of your prayer because you always receive an answer in one form or another. When I hear people express anxiety that a prayer has not yet been answered, I encourage them by mentioning to them that the answer is "on time" according to God's watch.

Every prayer, like David's Psalms, is a creation song, whose energy can go forth and attract that which is of like vibration and return it to you. In your prayer journal you can also keep a record of your prayer requests. Then re-read your requests in one or two month's time. You'll probably find, as I do, that you always got an answer. But the angels do not always answer your prayers in the way you expected. Sometimes the best answers are the ones which came in ways you didn't expect.

There have been a number of times that I never got what I prayed for, though I received an answer in another form. For example, where some external condition didn't change as I wanted it to, I found that I changed instead. In my own changing, I realized that the answer to my prayer was for my highest good and that, as always, Father knows best! So when you pray with the angels, live the full belief that your prayers will be answered. Miracles do happen, and prayers are the medium through which they occur.

In addition to individual prayer with the angels, I am also a firm believer in the power of angelic "prayer circles." A prayer circle is created when three or more people gather together to pray with the angels. There are actually many such established prayer healing circles throughout the world. One of the most powerful is the Angel Healing Circle located in Carmel, California, which has been operating continuously for twenty-one years. Group members at this location pray several times a day over the course of two weeks for the prayer requests supplied by people who phone or write them.

The prayer volunteers of Silent Unity in Unity Village, Missouri, pray in shifts around the clock. At any time and for any need, whether for yourself or another, you can call this organization and pray with someone over the phone. There were times during my marital separation when I needed the sound of a human voice praying with me to give me courage to get through the pain. When my divorce was finally behind me and I was experiencing the blessings and joys of a new relationship, I called the loving people at Unity to share this joy and gratitude with them in prayer.

A.R.E. Prayer Services is another group praying regularly for a variety of requests. The service is an ongoing project of A.R.E., which also sponsors the Glad Helpers Prayer Group, who have been meeting weekly in Virginia Beach, Virginia, since 1931. Formed at the request of Edgar Cayce himself, the group prays for and with individuals who request prayers for healing.

As an individual, you can enhance the power of your prayers by enlisting the aid of a prayer partner. Prayer partners are two people who agree to meet for prayer once a week for a predetermined amount of time. During such sessions, prayer partners pray with the angels by reading aloud written prayers that express their needs and the needs of others. Together, they ask the angels for God's guidance and assistance. Prayer partners can use established prayers or prayers that they write themselves. By their teaming up as a twosome in prayer, the Scriptural verse of Matthew 18:20 becomes a fulfilled promise, "For where two or three are gathered together in my name, there am I in the midst of them." Isn't that a glorious message of hope?

I have found that when I work with a prayer partner it enhances both our asking *and* our receiving. Just as it is good to have a companion who shares the same hobby or profession, it is a spiritually strengthening experience to work with a prayer friend. It's important to remember that you and your partner do not need to be together in the same place or even pray at the same time. In God's reality there is only the here and now. For myself, however, I prefer to be either at the same location or to have the mental link of designating a specific time when we are going to do our prayer work.

What kinds of requests can you make when you are praying with the angels? Anything and everything that is for your highest good and the highest good of all involved. When you pray with the angels, ask for your prayer to be fulfilled in that way. Life was meant to be a win/win proposition for everyone. So ask that the answers to your prayers be a blessing to all.

H.C. Moolenburgh in his book *A Handbook of Angels* states that when people pray, they not only personally receive grace but make their Guardian Angels happy.[4] So make an angel happy today—and *pray*!

Pray for help when you need it. Pray for comfort when you are feeling pain. When you are lost, pray for guidance as to which way to go. If you are on an important job interview, pray for clarity of thought. If you cannot locate something that you need, say a prayer for its return. When you need help *fast*, pray. Why go through something alone, when you have a multitude of angels with whom to pray? I believe that there is safety in numbers! That's why I always pray with the angels and they never let me down.

One of my dear friends refers to my angels as Janie's "Angel Patrol." He says that the "Angel Patrol" is always on the lookout when my family and friends are in need of help. Know that the "Angel Patrol" is there for you, too. When you need their assistance, you should just ask in prayer. But what about the formal prayers that we may have memorized as children—prayers we may never have fully understood? Is there any value to reciting them? I feel that there most definitely is! There have been many occasions of panic in my life where a recited prayer calmed me down and erased my fears.

Don't be overly anxious about the words you use when you are praying with the angels. Just go for it! Don't worry about where to pray because the angels are everywhere. If you need something, don't hesitate to ask for it through prayer. There's no need to struggle over whether or not you should pray for it. I can imagine the angels thinking, "I never thought you'd ask!" The right to ask is the gift of free will given to us by God. So it is important that if you want something, you ask for it.

One of Cayce's readings shares a delightful outlook on prayer: "...remember the injunction—never worry as long as you can pray. When you can't pray—you'd better begin to worry! For then you have something to worry about!" (3569-1)

Don't wait for the circumstances to be perfect to pray. Commit all your worries and problems to the angels through your prayers. It doesn't matter whether your request is large or small. The angels delight in hearing your prayers, in praying to God with you, and in doing good deeds in God's name.

Some Roman Catholics learn a prayer that beautifully reflects the role of the angels as messengers of God's love:

"Angels of God, who are my guardians, enlighten, guard, govern, and guide me who has been entrusted to you by the heavenly goodness. Amen."

There's no time that is not the right time for prayer. Even as I write this, I am saying a prayer for you that you, too, will experience the love of the angels by praying with them. If you feel alone, open your inner doors to the angels through prayer and let their love for you flow into your heart. When I pray with the angels, I always become aware of their presence in my life, and, therefore, I never feel alone. When I pray, a peace fills me through and through, and I feel God's presence even more.

What should you do after you have written down or released your prayer? In a small village in Pennsylvania in the 1800s, the following words were printed in a church bulletin:

"Pray for a good harvest, but keep on hoeing."

God and the angels will help you, but they also want you to do your part in answering your own prayers. Not only should you put your heart and soul into your prayers, you should put your hands and feet into them as well! Working goes hand-in-hand with praying.

The cooperation that you give God by taking an active role in answering your prayers is important. Your actions become part of the answer. Perhaps you are looking for a job. As you pray to be guided to your right place of employment, it may be that God will guide you there in a progression of steps. If you find you have to take an undesirable job, you may later discover that this job was the step that eventually led you to the place where you are eminently suited.

The Office of the Holy Tree of Life, published by the Sangreal Foundation,[5] lists a compendium of prayers for regular use by practicing kabbalists or followers of the Jewish mystical tradition known as kabbalah. Included among the many beautiful chants is the "Hymn of the Angels." I have used this chant as an invocation for my angel workshops because of the unmistakable feelings of love that the poetic words invoke when it is read in unison. There are ten verses to the chant, symbolic of the ten levels of divine reality. The hymn concludes with this verse:

> Fourfold Kerubim uphold us
> While we justify our birth
> Let the truth of life be told us
> As we listen on this Earth.

This hymn is a prayer-song honoring the angels. With the words "uphold us" we are asking the angels to support or help hold us up in times of struggle as we "justify our birth" or live out God's divine plan for us. "Let the truth of life be told us" is a request to the angels that the divine knowledge of God's truth be revealed to us. This verse thus encourages us to work hard to fulfill whatever our divine purpose is in life.

The chorus for the "Hymn of the Angels" reads: "Holy! Holy! Holy! Holy! Angels of the living tree." During my workshops, as the participants join in the chorus, we experience a powerful angelic essence that seems to flow from the throne of God. The feeling embraces each of the participants, connecting all of us with the angelic realm and the mystical Tree of Life to which it refers.

I want to share a personal story about a prayer that was answered by the angels in a most unusual way. While my husband and I were heading toward a divorce, all communication regarding negotiations over marital property had been relegated to our attorneys. Communicating with each other directly had become too painful.

I had been praying to the angels that the resolution of the divorce would be fair for both sides. I was also praying for a solution to the problem of where I was going to live. It soon appeared that the only way the issues would be resolved was by going to court.

At the time I had a dog named Rebel which I'd gotten as a puppy fifteen years earlier. Even though I had grown up with numerous dogs on my parents' farm, Rebel was the first dog who belonged only to me and I adored her. She was a combination schnauzer and poodle—a snoodle of a dog! She loved to go swimming with me in my parents' country pond and would especially love the times when she would sit in an aqua-chair and I would act as the motor and paddle her around the perimeter of the pond. I had taught Rebel to carry her own mini beach towel. She would lead the way across a wooden bridge to the pond with her towel in her mouth. Then she'd drop it by the pier and joyfully be the first one in the water for a refreshing swim.

By the time of my separation, she had lost her hearing and had become partially blind and lame. Rebel had been a dear companion to me through the separation experience. Even with her physical limitations, she always "sensed" when I came home from work and would be there to greet me.

On the fifteenth anniversary of her coming into my life fog shrouded the neighborhood. Rebel went outside as she usually did in the evening, but when I went to let her back in, I couldn't find her. I called for what seemed like hours, even though I knew she couldn't hear me. I searched the entire neighborhood, but she was nowhere to be found. It was as if she had vanished. The fog only added to the frustration of not being able to find her. I prayed with the angels for her safe return.

The next morning, as soon as the fog lifted, my parents

joined me in my frantic search for Rebel. Since we live in a rural area, we were surrounded by fields and pastures. We walked everywhere looking for any trace of Rebel. I put notices in mailboxes and hung signs on telephone poles. I notified the humane society. I called the local newspaper and ran a Lost Dog ad. Then, I received a phone call.

The call came from a nearby farmer. The farmer had seen one of my signs. Rebel, who could hardly walk, had wandered about a mile from home and down the long driveway of this farm. The way she had staggered into this farm, the owner feared that she might be a threat to his horses and cattle. She had no tags because she was a house dog who never ventured outside of my five acres of land. Because of the farm owner's fear that my dog could be rabid, he destroyed Rebel within a few hours of her arrival on his farm without questioning anyone in the community as to whom she might belong.

I was devastated over the loss of my beloved companion. I felt that if someone had shown me a door marked, "This way out of life," I would have entered it. Going through the experience of separation, compounded by the loss of my beloved Rebel, I felt the pain had reached a point that I just couldn't bear.

I remember praying with the angels that Rebel be kept in their good care, and I tried to comfort myself with the notion that she was finally able to see, hear, run, and swim in a heavenly pond again. But I missed her and knew I would feel the loss every time I walked through the back door of my home expecting her to greet me.

A week's time passed and I received an unexpected phone call at my office. Through the family grapevine, my former spouse had learned of Rebel's death and had called to express his sadness over it. That conversation was our first verbal exchange in two years, and a profound healing occurred between us. We both agreed that somewhere along the line things had gotten crazy between us, and we both expressed our desire to resolve the marital property issues, to finalize the divorce, and to get on with our lives. Prior to hanging up the phone, I said, "I want to thank you for calling and I really want to thank Rebel for what she did, too."

I am a believer that all the kingdoms work together for God's divine plan. I believe that Rebel knew that it was time for her to make her transition. She knew that I was not capable of making the decision of having her put to sleep. Instinctively she went to a place where it would be done quickly. In her final act on the earth plane she worked hand in hand with the angels in answering my prayers. With the angels' help, Rebel gave me the gift of healing in my life. In honor of Rebel and the glorious angels, I renamed my property. For fifteen years we had called it "Tulip Poplar Hill"; now my home is called "Angel Heights."

·CRIS ARBO·

Chapter Five

Share with the Angels

"The Lord, before whom I walk, will send his angel with thee, and prosper thy way . . . "
Genesis 24:40

Robert Fulghum in his book, *All I Really Need to Know I Learned in Kindergarten,* said that one of the most important things he learned was to "share everything."[1] To share is to allow others to participate in whatever you're doing. You can share your time in talking with others. You can share your energy by doing for others. You can share your resources by giving to others.

Whenever I share—whether it be sharing myself in conversation or sharing an experience, such as going to a concert with someone—I find that the activity becomes a three-dimensional occurrence: I experience the event from my perspective, from the perspective of my companion, and from the perspective of our sharing it together. I believe the combination of our experience creates its own unique perspective. When I share, I experience the joy of both giving and receiving, as the old proverb states: "A sorrow that's shared is but half a trouble, but a joy that's shared is a joy made double."

I feel that sharing is an important ingredient in maintaining a healthy life. Rev. Bruce Larson in his book, *There's a Lot More to Health Than Not Being Sick,* states: "To know and be known is a vital ingredient for physical and spiritual wholeness. It is a medical, psychological, and spiritual fact that people who need people (and who know it) are the luckiest people in the world. I suppose this is why the human race has historically lived in tribes and then in villages."[2]

Sharing is a natural part of our existence. We are one with God, and God shares His life force with us. We are one with all creation and share the same origin. We all come from God, and we are all members of God's family. God is our Father/Mother, and we are brothers and sisters to the angels.

There is a helpful word that I feel is unfortunately dropping from our vocabulary due to lack of usage. I just don't hear people saying it, and I hope that my book changes the lost status of this word. The word is *fellowship.* Fellowship is communing with others. In fellowship we come together and share.

The Greek root for the word *fellowship* is "koinonia," which means "common." The word *common* means "belonging to all." So when we share or participate in fellowship, we are experiencing what we have in common. When you share your life with the angels, you experience that you "belong to the all"; what you have in common with the angels is God's love. The word *commune* originates from the Latin "communis," which means "common." Sharing your life is another way to commune with the angels and establish fellowship with them.

"Fellowship" is one of twelve lessons in spiritual development worked with in the Edgar Cayce Search for God Study Group program. It is included in chapter 6 of *A Search for God,* Book I, one of two texts used for group study. Participants in such groups attempt to apply fellowship in their daily lives.

Between the moments you spend meditating and the periods of prayer in your life, you have many opportunities to share your life with the angels. I encourage you to share your whole life with them and draw them into whatever you are doing. The angels will become involved, connected, and included in your life. The more you share with the angels, the easier it becomes to relate to them and to operate with their help because you have given yourself yet another opportunity to get to know them. So if you desire to have a close relationship with the angels, start by sharing the activities of your life with them.

Take a look at the world today. It is as if people are walking around wearing "Do not disturb" signs. Joggers wear headsets that isolate them in a world of their own. High fences go up between homes, and some of us use answering machines so we don't have to talk with others. People riding on elevators often make no eye contact. Some fear smiling at strangers because the smile may be misinterpreted. I feel there's a real need for healing in our involvement with others on this planet. I feel that we need fellowship with each other as well as with the angels.

By communing with the angels, you can open yourself to the experience of being a "share-and-share alike" person. This means that you share what you have with the angels, and they share what they have with you in mutual cooperation. The experience will fill your life with blessings, the more you share. After all, we are kindred spirits with the angels because we were all created together in the beginning.

I encourage you to include the angels in your work and play, your happy times and sad times, your ups and downs. When you open your eyes in the morning, welcome the angels into your world. Share with them the joy of being blessed with another new day of life on the earth and acknowledge that they will be with you during all your experiences of the day. When you go to sleep at night, give thanks to them for watching over you during the day. Ask them for the blessing of a good night's sleep.

One of the best examples of how sharing my life with the angels has helped me is the story of how I came to do my angel workshops. I've done over 100 workshops now over the past five years, but if the angels hadn't saved me from myself, I may never have found my calling. "Saving us from ourselves" seems to be an angelic specialty. We are often our own worst enemies. By sharing our lives with the angels, we give them the opportunity to show us how to avoid our own trap doors, land mines, and self-created fire hazards. I would like to mention an especially humorous story of how the angels rescued me from myself.

In those days, two years before my marriage ended, I was in the midst of an intense search for myself, for the truth, and for a practical way to use my resources to help others. But like many seekers nowadays with the upsurge of various spiritual movements and "new thought" organizations, I was soon extending myself beyond the limits of my ability to absorb it all.

I had spent the previous year reading books—sometimes four at once. I had attended seminars on everything—from aborigine healing techniques to bending silver spoons with my mind. I wanted to know everything there was to know about paranormal phenomena and I wanted to know it NOW. I learned about meditating, clearing the chakras, astral traveling, sending absentee healing, and frankly my mind was swimming. I functioned by day in the business world of advertising and at night enrolled in workshops where I learned how to function with equal comfort in the spirit world. I joked that one morning I was going to answer the office phone with "Good morning. What is your astrological sign?" In sharing this story as part of my workshop lecture, so many people have commented on having had the same experience: an unquenchable thirst to learn everything there is to know, metaphysically speaking.

One day in meditation, I received a clear message from the angels. It came to me in a vision displayed on the screen of my inner mind. It showed me that what I needed to do was to follow the example of Jesus. I needed to fast from all the books, tapes, and workshops. The angels advised me to follow Jesus' wisdom and spend forty days in the wilderness of my mind to assimilate all the material I had been studying. Furthermore, they said that if I didn't do this, I was going to burn out. But did I listen?

One Thursday evening, I had just finished my work at a recording studio for the advertising agency where I was employed. While heading home, I suddenly felt that I'd been told by the angels to go back to the office and unload the car. I questioned their advice because I planned to go to the office first thing the next morning. Also it was almost "quitting time." But the angels persisted. I followed their suggestion and drove to the office, after stopping for gas. My co-workers commented on how ridiculous it was to come back to the office so late since they were all heading out the door. I shrugged, unloaded the car, and drove home. After parking the car, I went inside. Moments later,

I happened to look out my front door and saw to my horror the front of my Jeep engulfed in flames.

At that time in my life I was not especially adept at handling crises. I quickly dialed 411—which was the number for directory information. The operator told me to hang up and try 911, which I did immediately.

While waiting for the fire truck to arrive, I remembered running around my flaming Jeep in panicked circles wondering what to do. Suddenly, I sensed a formation of angels building a wall around the Jeep. I was told to step back, take a deep breath, and be as calm as possible until the fire truck arrived.

The firemen arrived in record time; however, the Jeep was totally burnt underneath the hood. The insurance company's investigation revealed that the accident had been caused by loose wires. They said that never in the history of the company had they seen a car burned in a fire of that intensity without exploding in flames. The car dealership where I bought the Jeep wanted to rebuild it from scratch rather than "total" it as a lost cause. I was all for the decision, as I knew that I could read a message for myself in what happened to my Jeep: that in our spiritual fervor we can burn ourselves out from relentless seeking. Having lost "my wheels" due to the fire incident, I was restricted in my ability to travel to workshops. In fact, I did follow the message of the vision and for forty days enrolled in no classes. I read no books during that time, nor did I listen to any tapes. I allowed myself to spend time in meditation and prayer and communing with nature. I took advantage of this opportunity to process everything I had learned, and to think about how I could take all my experiences and accumulation of information and give something back to the world. I prayed to God for His will to be made known to me.

It took exactly forty days to rebuild the Jeep. As the fortieth day approached, the angels joyously shared with me the message that I should apply for a "vanity" license plate that says WE ARE ONE. It wasn't long after the fortieth day that they told me, "It is time to get off your horizon and shine." I was encouraged to develop my angel workshops, which five years later I have given at conferences, institutes, centers, and private homes throughout the country. I was given the inspiration to be a messenger for the angels—and I'm happy to report that my Jeep is still running beautifully.

Because we are all inveterate seekers, I know that when I am 101 years old, I'll still be signing up for workshops and buying the latest spiritual book. The angels, however, have taught me balance in my life. There is a time to give out information and a time to receive it, a time to work and a time to play and a time to rest. Share all these experiences with the angels. They are your beautiful helpmates who will assist you in finding the path of balance in your life.

Sometimes the angels give you answers by leading you to messages in books. It's just one more way in which they can help you if you share your life with them. Often, the form these messages take can be very dramatic.

During the summer of 1991, I remember feeling completely overwhelmed. My schedule was jam-packed with working a full-time job, conducting workshops, attending conferences, lecturing, and giving readings. My life had become unbalanced, as I wasn't taking off to relax or spend time with the new man in my life. Whenever anyone asked for my help, I wasn't able to say "no"—even to help myself. One of my friends referred to me as Janie Big Heart. I shared all of this with the angels and asked for help.

The angels showed me a vision of myself as a little mermaid. I felt a sadness come over me as I connected with this mermaid. I slowly became aware that I didn't have any legs. I couldn't dance or play with the prince that I had seen on shore. From deep within me came the interpretation: The sadness I was feeling came from my not making time for the new love—this new "prince of a man"—in my life.

One particular weekend this very special person had invited me to attend a family party, but I had to decline because of my prior commitment to a weekend conference about a two-hour drive away. Just before I left for the conference, my friend once again mentioned that, if the opportunity presented itself, even late, the family would love to have me join them. Once again, I felt the sadness of that mermaid.

I went to the conference and gave my workshop on Friday afternoon, again that evening, and then again on Saturday afternoon. But following the Saturday afternoon workshop, I noticed that a block of time had suddenly opened up. I was free from Saturday evening until Sunday morning, when I would have to give the workshop again. I asked the angels, "Please show me if I am to drive back to Maryland and attend the party?" I didn't "hear" a response, so I resigned myself to remain there, rationalizing that it was just too much driving. Attending the party would entail driving home, then returning early Sunday morning to be available for my next workshop.

Suddenly I found myself sitting in the library of the metaphysical organization sponsoring the conference. Before me was a pile of books and a sign which read, "Free to Whoever Wants Them." Absently, I took one of the books, an illustrated children's book. It fell open to a picture of a little mermaid. The message was clear to me. I had been shown what I needed to do for my highest good: to get into my car and go to the party. I finally went home to play, and the angels played right along with me.

If you but share your life with them, the angels will also help you overcome your self-imposed limitations. During my eighteen years of marriage, I never did any long-distance driving myself. I would usually ride along and enjoy the scenery on any long-distance trips. After my divorce, however, I found myself in the unfamiliar role of long-distance driver. I remember sharing with the angels all my fears about driving outside of familiar territory. I was afraid of having my car break down and afraid of getting lost. The more I thought about it, the more I convinced myself that I couldn't drive long distances to do workshops.

My fears resulted in my turning down any work that required long-distance driving—which, to me, was any-thing over an hour. I shared with the angels that in my heart I didn't want to be limited in where I lectured, but I couldn't seem to get over this hurdle of fear.

A good friend of mine, Gabrielle, who lives a three-hour drive away, kept asking me to come and conduct a work-shop. I had established a following there prior to my separation, and the people wanted me to return. The location was not near any bus or train station, so if I was going to do it, I was going to have to drive. I still balked.

The angels started giving me messages that it was nec-essary for my growth to overcome my fear and go give this workshop. It was time for me to let go of my self-imposed limitation, claim my wings, and fly out of my neighbor-hood.

I was receiving support from the angelic realm and from my earth angel friend, Gabrielle, as well. Her name is appropriate, as she is an exemplification of the message, "God is my strength." Gabrielle outlined the following plan: I would leave work early and drive up on a Friday afternoon to avoid all the rush-hour traffic in my area as well as hers. I would let my family know when I was leaving and, if anything happened in the first one-and-a-half hours' drive, they would come to get me. If anything happened from that point forward, Gabrielle and her husband would take care of me. Additionally, she sent me explicit directions. The plan gave me the assurance I needed that I wasn't making this trip alone, as well as put my mind to rest about getting lost or wondering what would happen if my car broke down. Though with some hesitation on my part and the urging of the angels, I agreed.

When the day of my trek arrived, however, my boss accidently backed into my car and crunched my grill. I was convinced that this was a sign that I wasn't to go. My fear jumped at the opportunity to find a way out. My boss, who was aware of the importance of my reclaiming my wings, said, "If your car doesn't run, you'll take my BMW. One way or another, you are going!"

As it turned out, the damage done to my car was insignificant, and so off I drove. At first I was terrified, but as I drove the fear gradually left me. The longer I drove, the more I loved it. It was a wonderfully freeing experience.

As Gabrielle waited for my arrival, she told me later she saw a vision of my car coming into her driveway but in a direction opposite to the usual flow of traffic. She immediately knew that the angels were giving her a sign that I would make it without any problem. When I arrived, I followed the pattern she saw in her vision earlier.

After that weekend, I became a frequent traveler on the roads of the East Coast. The angels and Gabrielle helped me develop my wings so that I could spread the word. It all resulted from my sharing my fears with the angels.

Too often people think of the angels as solemn beings. I have found in my work and in my life that they love parties and celebrations, and welcome the invitation to not only participate but to share in the planning of them as well.

In August of 1987, I decided to open my home one weekend to anyone who wanted to celebrate a cosmic event known as the Harmonic Convergence. This event had been predicted by the Mayans to take place on August 16 and 17, 1987. It was promoted nationally by Colorado mystic Jose Arguelles. I had received confirmation in meditation with the angels that this was a major planetary event and that I was to participate. I knew that the energy would be intense that weekend and that nothing would be better than to close our celebration on Sunday with a song. We needed something that would prepare us for going back to work on Monday morning. Oftentimes when participating in spiritual retreat weekends, I find that I have the experience of being in another world, so the transition back to the business world is rather jolting. But what was the song to be?

I suggested to a friend who was helping me plan the weekend that we go into meditation and ask for the name of a song that we could use for the closing ceremony. My friend, who was also long-practiced at communing with the angels, did just that and received the message immediately that the song should be the theme from *Ghostbusters*, a movie that was popular at that time. When he shared this with me, I have to admit that I was somewhat suspicious about what angel would have supplied such an answer. I even remarked that he should ask again.

The next day, I was shown a humorous vision of my being surrounded by angels wearing party hats and tooting horns. After doing a double take, I asked what was going on. The angels informed me that they were giving me the message that there was a celebration of rebirth taking place on the earth and that the Harmonic Convergence was an important part of that celebration. They also

added that my friend was correct—the song should be the
theme from *Ghostbusters*. They went on to instruct me that
where the words of the song asked, "Who you gonna call?"
when you are in need of assistance, rather than answering
"Ghostbusters," the group was to sing "Lightworkers." It's
not ghosts but lightworkers who are answering God's call
to be volunteers on the earth plane.

The two-day Harmonic Convergence celebration at my
home was a weekend filled with meditation, prayer, and
fellowship. Many of us that weekend received messages
from the angels that we were being awakened to serve God
with an unshakable new commitment. It was a cosmic
moment during which we felt a new beginning —one that
was being ushered in with the help of the angels.

Sunday evening, when the weekend drew to a close, the
song from *Ghostbusters* was played. It was a joyous experience as we shouted out our names—"Lightworkers"! Singing the song was a healing in itself and, as we sang, all the
wonderful messages of the weekend seemed to be anchored within us. We were finally prepared to return to our
jobs the next morning to spread the light and love received
from the angels, who participated with us in this celestial
and planetary event.

What the angels do best when you share your life with
them is to give you little clues about what is going to
happen in your life. Years later, when you reflect upon the
clues, you might be overwhelmed as to the help that's been
available to you.

Some years ago I participated in a workshop on
mediumship and development of psychic ability. We were
taught exercises and techniques to receive messages from
spirit guides and guardians as well as from angels. I
remember a young woman named Mary Jane who sat next
to me in the class. We instantly liked each other even

though we had never met before.

I had already taken numerous workshops on communicating with spirits, but I took this class because I had tremendous respect for the instructor. Years earlier, she had given me my first clue, through her spirit guides, that I would one day be a communicator between the earth and the higher realms. She did not tell me that message to flatter me but rather to emphasize the importance of my beginning immediately to develop myself for the role if I chose to accept it.

Through years of regular meditation and prayer, I had developed the ability to receive messages easily. This instructor had encouraged me to practice, practice, practice. She told me to join a weekly group in which I would have the opportunity to give messages. I worked very hard in fine-tuning my communication skills. As I watched myself grow from one who was uncertain about the messages I was receiving into a confident intuitive reader, I also grew into the realization that I wanted to communicate messages from the angels.

Over the course of this two-day workshop, Mary Jane made the comment that she wanted to "be like me," because it was her impression that I was fluent in communicating with the higher realms. I told her that in time she, too, would be fluent and that the angels told me she would be communicating chiefly through art—drawing for others what their spirit guides and angels looked like.

From that first meeting with Mary Jane a friendship grew. She continued to grow spiritually, but didn't start drawing angels until one Saturday morning in July, 1990. She was in her apartment meditating when she received an urgent message from the angels: get your drawing materials and draw "Janie's angel." She heard the message clearly, "It is important that Janie see her angel."

Mary Jane did as she was instructed. Several hours later, when the drawing was finished, she called me saying that she had something to show me. She asked if she could come to my home. The day she had received the message to draw my angel she couldn't have known that I had just received the divorce papers and was praying to the angels for support. I had no idea what it was she had to show me. Then, she presented me with her gift. It was a colorful painting of an angel with hands raised, facing outward to bless me when I stood before it. It now hangs in my hallway and blesses all who enter my home.

I was moved by the fact that the angels had contacted Mary Jane on my behalf and also moved because several years earlier I had been told that she would draw angels and that mine would be the first. I see the experience now as a perfect example of the universality of the angels' knowledge. The painting is to this day a cogent reminder to me of their support and of the many ways they communicate their messages to us whenever we share our lives with them.

The angels especially enjoy being messengers of love. The "cupids" traditionally associated with St. Valentine's Day deliver love messages all year round. I had an experience that demonstrates this.

Following my divorce, I was awakened one night from sleep by a loud knocking on the front door. I opened the door, but no one was there. Had it been a spiritual knock? I went into meditation and asked the angels what it meant. I was told to be ready, because "someone" would soon be coming into my life. I shrugged it off and went back to sleep.

My home is located in the beautiful rolling farm country of Maryland. Periodically, the local hound and hunt club traipses through the property. One Saturday afternoon, not too long after the strange knocking on the front door, I stepped onto my front porch and saw one of the leaders of the hunt standing underneath my immense 200-year-old tulip poplar tree. He was smartly dressed in a riding habit and was carrying a hunters' horn under his arm. I knew that he was pausing to allow for the regrouping of the hounds. The moment I saw him, however, I heard the angels say, "This is another message. There will be a man coming into your life." I have to admit that by that time they had stimulated my curiosity.

I shared these two messages with a friend of mine and also the hope that I might soon be meeting someone. My friend, who was especially adept psychically, tended to focus on cosmic or global symbols. She was a bit skeptical when I said I thought the messages were for me. With a wave of her hand, she said, "I don't think the messages were necessarily for you personally. They're probably symbolic of the new thoughts coming to the earth now. The knocking was to tell all the lightworkers that a new door is opening, and the man with the horn was a symbol of the heralding in of a new era."

Needless to say, my bubble was burst. I wanted the messages to be for me. Later that morning I shared with the angels, "You know how much I believe in the blessing of the Trinity and the power of three. Give me a third sign that will show me that the messages were for me. And don't make it so metaphysical that it can be misinterpreted as a message for the world. How about one that will make me laugh." I heard an etheric response, "Consider it done."

About a week later it was my birthday. One of my high school friends had sent me a helium-filled balloon in the shape of a banana man with dangling arms and legs. I placed the banana man in the dining room with other balloons I had received earlier.

That evening, the woman who had interpreted my messages as global rather than personal came to my house to join me for some healing meditative work. I wanted to show her the banana-man balloon but, as I looked into the dining room, I couldn't find it. I assumed that he had lost his air and was now residing on the floor underneath the table. I just forgot about him and I looked no further.

As I was straightening up after my friend's departure, I got curious as to where the balloon was. I thoroughly searched the dining room and the entire downstairs, but there was no sign of it. I finally tracked him down, though, when I went to bed that night. He greeted me, straddled over the top of my armoire. I laughed until my sides ached. It wouldn't have been so funny, except that I live in a two-story house. In order for the banana-man balloon to have found his way to my room, he would have had to float through the dining room, out through the living room, turn a corner, and travel up a flight of stairs. At the top of the stairs, he would have to choose among three rooms, somehow make a sharp right turn into the master bedroom, and position himself in an ungentlemanly pose atop a tall piece of furniture. I finally realized that the banana-man balloon was the third sign that someone wonderful was on his way.

After my laugh, I asked the angels, "How am I going to know this man?" The angels said that they would point him out to me. With that assurance I didn't think any more about the banana-man.

Nearly a month later, I was giving mini-readings at a fair hosted by a local metaphysical book store when a man whom I'd never met before asked me for a reading. He was impressed with the session and asked if he could have a longer session. I scheduled an appointment for him to have an extended session in my home office.

Just before his session, I had felt guided to bring into my office a statue of Archangel Michael, which I had purchased in Mexico several months before. I placed it behind the chair where this man would be sitting.

For one hour I gave the man messages from his Guardian Angel and other angels of service. It was a session like none I had ever done before. It was difficult for me to remain focused because I felt extremely warm, as if there was an energy drawing me toward the man's heart. At the end of the session I asked him if he had any questions. He said he had one. He shared that he was a widower and wanted to know if he would ever have a love life again. At that moment I saw the statue of Archangel Michael "come to life" in my imagination and point his sword at this man. I pride myself on the professionalism of my work, so I simply remarked that he should just make his request known to the angels. I told him that I was certain someone would be on her way soon.

The next evening, while dining with my girlfriend Mary, I shared the experience I had had the night before. Her first question was, "Well, aren't you going to ask him out?" I realized that I was blushing as I responded that this man was twenty-six years older than I. Mary took on the teacher role as she commented, "I don't believe it. You are always telling people to have no limitations, and here you are letting age limit you." She was right. In about two weeks' time I mustered up enough nerve to call him. We talked, one thing led to another, and we went on our first date the very next day. The relationship has continued to grow into one of commitment, support, and love for each other. I call this wonderful person my "Angel Man," as he truly was sent from the angels. I had left it up to the angels to bring this man into my life, right through the front door where the spiritual knock was first heard and into my office which overlooks my tulip poplar tree.

I also want to share a message that this man was given during his initial mini-reading which was repeated in the one-hour session. He had had a near-death experience during surgery a year prior to my meeting him. He had not told me that; the angels did. When I said to him, "You made the decision to come back," he added, "because there were things I needed to finish." I corrected him as the angels said, "No, there is something you need to begin." Not only did this man come back to begin a relationship with me that provided a beautiful healing in my life, but he later fulfilled his lifelong dream of building a vacation home on a beautiful five-acre tract in West Virginia.

This reminds me of one of my favorite angel stories which involves Michaelangelo, the Renaissance artist. One day he saw a block of marble that he wanted to carve. But the owner said it had no value. Michaelangelo immediately said that it had value to him, because there was an angel imprisoned inside it that he had to set free. There is an angel imprisoned inside every one of our dreams, and only we can set it free by giving it life—as did Michaelangelo and this man who built his dream house which now blesses all who come to it.

I think one of the keys to having an intimate relationship with the angels is not to censor the thoughts and words that you share. Too often people think that because of the angels' heavenly vibration, they should only be included in activities that have a PG rating: "perfect and good." Even though I am aspiring to experience my highest good, there are many times when I have felt in a sour mood, angry, or perplexed. Even so, I realize those are the times when I especially need the support of the angels, who always give me space to have my snit fits and then lovingly intervene and say, "Enough is enough, Janie," encouraging me to take some positive action to free myself from my negative mood.

The angels have shared with me one of the most important tests that can be given in spiritual growth. I call it "The Emperor Has No Clothes" test. You may find yourself sometime at a lecture or a workshop, and discover that the information being given does not ring true for you. It does not necessarily mean that the information is right or wrong. It simply means that it is not your truth. You need to know that it is all right to say, "This isn't my truth," and walk away. Just as the little boy in the fairy tale of "The Emperor Has No Clothes" spoke out and declared that the Emperor was stark naked when everyone else was pretending he was clothed, there are times in our lives when we have to acknowledge we don't see what others see. It is truly an empowering moment because you are claiming what is truth for you.

The angels are wonderful at helping you find information whenever you share a need. They can send messages through books, as they did for me with the mermaid story, but they can use any tool that you give them to help you.

One evening I was with several girlfriends, one of whom was struggling with a message on humility that she had received from the I-Ching. The woman was questioning why, after years of working on being able to assert herself, she was being asked to be humble. We sought further explanation beyond what was given by the I-Ching, and the angels prompted me to go to the dictionary and follow the path down which the Latin origin would lead.

I looked up the word *humility* and found the Latin word "humilitas" with the comment "akin to humus." I looked up *humus*, which means "soil's organic part," and discovered that it was akin to "homage." I looked up *homage*, which means "showing respect or allegiance to one's lord."

The angels immediately chimed in by telling me that, when we are asked to be humble, we are being asked to show respect and allegiance to God.

Humility is recognizing that we are akin not only to the earth but to all life. When we recognize that oneness, it helps us to become aware of our own inner magnificence. Rather than being lowered through humility, we are actually lifted up to share our rightful place as sons and daughters of God. Waiting to welcome us to these, our places of honor, are the glorious angels.

The angels have been as helpful to me when I need to find lost objects as they are in helping me find answers. They can be super detectives. I remember one Christmas when I was decorating my house and couldn't find my wooden folk-art duck. At the Christmas season I always had placed a scotch-plaid bow around the duck's neck and displayed it in the living room. The rest of the year, though, he would sit unadorned in the den. But dressing him up for Christmas was one of my holiday rituals. I searched the house high and low. The duck was not to be found.

I asked the angels to give me guidance on where I had put the duck. They inexplicably responded, "He's not in the house." I immediately thought, "What a crazy answer. Of course, he's in the house." I continued my madness of rummaging through closets, peering under beds, but no duck hiding place was discovered.

Finally one day I thought I would ask the cleaning woman who comes in once a week if she had noticed where I had put it. The woman responded apologetically, almost to the point of tears, that in her cleaning she had broken the duck and had taken it home for her husband to fix. So it was true that the duck wasn't in the house. I could have sworn I heard an angelic, "We told you so."

I love hearing stories of how angels have touched others'

lives and shared God's wisdom when these people shared their problems with the angels. One of my favorites was told to me by a woman who'd had a distressing confrontation with her teen-age daughter right before my workshop. Her daughter wanted to spend the upcoming evening at a girlfriend's house, but the mother wasn't comfortable about this particular friend, feeling that she had an unhealthy influence on her daughter.

During one of the guided meditations in the workshop, I suggested that each participant silently share her problems with the angels and then listen for the message that was given. This woman stated her fears, and then heard only one word, "Trust."

The woman went home, and before her daughter left for her friend's house, she shared what had taken place at the workshop and the one-word message she had received. She and her daughter had a long-needed healing conversation about what the message of trust had meant to each of them. As a result, they discovered a vital common ground that had been missing in their relationship. By sharing their lives with the angels, mother and daughter established a meeting point of honor and mutual respect. The daughter left knowing that she was trusted and responded to that trust by making wiser, more responsible decisions about her friends and activities. The mother found an inner peace in trusting that even when she is not with her daughter, her child is "entrusted" to the care of the angels.

There's one more story I want to tell you as part of this chapter on sharing your life with the angels. It is the story about this book. It is an important story as it beautifully illustrates the angels' love for you and how much they want to communicate with you.

During the summer of 1991 I attended the Rainbow Spectrum Conference, a week-long metaphysical confer-

ence, in Elizabethtown, Pennsylvania, where I led workshops and lectured. During my week's stay I treated myself
to an intuitive reading.

The woman who gave me the reading told me that
within one year I would have a book published. I had no
plans to write a book at that time, nor did I have any
unpublished manuscripts sitting on my desk. I remarked
to her that I didn't know what I would possibly write about
in such a short amount of time. She asked me where I
obtained the information for my angel workshops, which
she had found very helpful. I commented that a lot of it
came directly from the angels themselves. I said to her,
"The angels tell me what to say." She smiled and said,
"And they will tell you what to write in the book."

Shortly after that reading, as a member of the Association for Research and Enlightenment (A.R.E.), I received
information on the Association's bi-monthly paranormal
experiment. This particular project was a survey of members' experiences with angels. I was thrilled to see the
research that was being done on the angels, so I wrote the
A.R.E. and complimented them on their topic choice. I also
enclosed several magazine articles that I had written about
the angels.

I received a phone call from one of the editors of A.R.E.
Press asking if I would consider submitting a proposal on
a book about the angels. I didn't know if I could because I'd
never written a book before, but I heard a supportive, "Yes,
we can do this!" from the angels. I agreed to write such a
proposal to A.R.E. Press within two weeks' time. I sat at the
computer and with the angels' help wrote my book proposal.

The proposal moved quickly through the necessary
channels at A.R.E. Press and in January 1992 I received a
contract to write this book. The contract arrived in time to

be part of my forty-first birthday celebration.

I was told repeatedly by the angels as I sat at my computer, "There're some people waiting to read your words. Tell them we love them!" I hope you are one of those who was waiting for this book.

My relationship with the angels has grown even closer and more endearing through the writing. It has been a beautiful sharing experience for me.

There is so much joy that you can experience by sharing your life with the angels, so go ahead. Try it. Share your life with the angels for a week, and see what happens. Make a card or tie a string around your finger to help you remember to share. Old habits are hard to break, but it can be done. You can change the habit of keeping everything to yourself and start sharing with the angels right now.

Open yourself up to the angels and you can find that you are opening yourself up to God, to heaven and all of its healing, illumination, and love. Allow yourself to feel the bond between you and your angel for it will grow from this special moment when you decide to share your life with your celestial best friend, your Guardian Angel. Let yourself feel your angel encircle you with love and give you a healing hug. Feel yourself reciprocate. Let your love flow to your angel. Have fellowship with your friends, the angels, and share yourself!

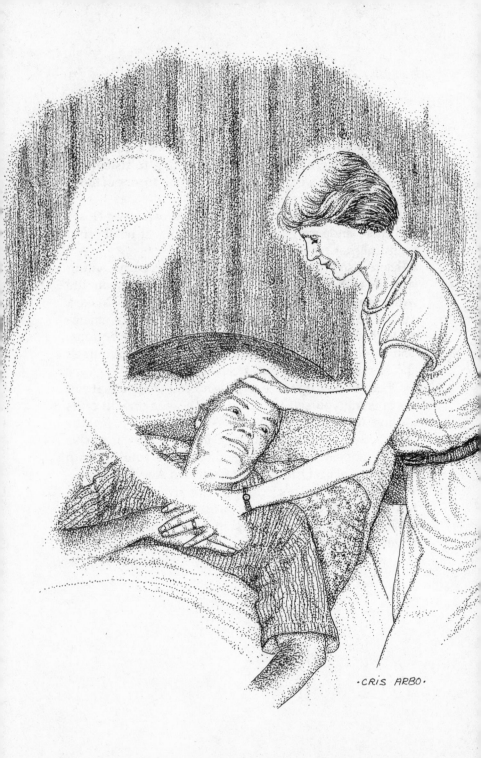

·CRIS ARBO·

Chapter Six

Healing with the Angels

*"Behold, I send an Angel before thee, to keep thee in
the way, and to bring thee into the place
which I have prepared."*
Exodus 23:20

The angels provide that unseen hand that reaches out to
guide us, protect us, and heal us. Sometimes the world
appears to be a dark, cold place but it can be lighted and
warmed by the lamps of love carried by the angels. With
their radiant energy they can even light the path to healing
in often surprising ways.

One of my workshop participants, Margaret, shared
with me how she had at one time been very sick with
bronchitis, which turned into pneumonia, and then wors-
ened. Weeks later, even after faithful visits to the doctors,
numerous examinations, tests, and antibiotics, she

remained very ill. There seemed to be a missing ingredient in her healing.

One evening, Margaret had a dream in which she clearly saw herself and just how weak her physical body had become. She saw a beautiful band of healing angels lift her from the bed and beckon her to go with them "to a place of healing." As she observed herself with them, Margaret felt strengthened by their aid.

The next morning, as she drove to her doctor's appointment, she remembered the dream and how the angels had supported her. Suddenly, she thought she heard a voice. "Make an appointment with the angels," it said. She heard the words distinctly, and she remembered being startled. Yet the message had been crystal clear.

That evening she followed the directions of her traditional medical doctor in taking the prescribed medicine. But she also gave herself some uninterrupted time for meditation in order to keep her appointment with the angels and go "to a place of healing," as they had requested in her dream. So she lay down and went into a deep meditation.

During that appointment with the angels, Margaret recalled feeling the strong, loving support of the angels' presence. She immediately sensed she was not alone in her desire to be healed. She visualized the angels taking her to a place which she described as a "healing garden." As she sat on a beautiful marble bench in this garden, a brilliant rainbow appeared in the sky, springing from the very place where she was seated. Margaret found herself being showered with a multicolored radiance. She felt that a magical, divine alchemy was working within her. After an unknown lapse of time, she was finally "returned to her bed" from the healing garden. In the morning, the angels encouraged her to open her eyes and heart with great expectation for what turned out to be a joyous day ahead of her.

That had been for Margaret the first of many profound appointments with the angels. She would listen for their advice each day and it came with astonishing variety. The angels' suggestions included the advice to have a happy, loving attitude so that joy would lift her up above her illness. The angels spoke of happy people being healthy people. One day she was encouraged to do breathing exercises and to spend time outside to breathe in lots of fresh air. Another day she was told to rest longer, and on another to do visualizations of seeing healing energy pouring into her body from the angelic realm.

Margaret fully recovered in six weeks' time. She credits her recovery to the energy and advice of the angels who, she believes, nurtured her back to health. Of course, they were only able to do it through divine guidance and through her willingness to listen. She admits that her healing was assisted by the medical prescriptions, but that the prescriptions alone had not been enough.

Victor Hugo is given credit for the words "Go to sleep in peace. God is awake." That is such a lovely expression of support and protection, not only for our sleeping but also our waking hours. God is always with us and has given us the service of the angels, if we only ask for it.

Padre Pio of Pietrelcina was an Italian Catholic priest in the early part of this century who experienced the phenomenon of the stigmata—the visible signs of Christ's crucifixion appearing on his hands and feet. He is currently being considered for beatification by the Roman Catholic church. Throughout his writings are stories of his own personal experiences with the angels as well as those shared by his parishioners. In the biography *Send Me Your Guardian Angel, Padre Pio,* Fr. Alessio Parente writes, "Padre Pio's spiritual guidance of souls was mostly done through the help and direction of his Guardian Angel."[1] In a letter written on April 20, 1915, Padre Pio wrote, "What a consolation it is to know one is always in the care of a celestial spirit, who does not abandon us . . . "[2]

Padre Pio would receive letters from all over the world that had been written in languages unknown to him. Miraculously, through the assistance of his Guardian Angel, these letters would instantaneously be translated in his mind as he read them. A parish priest who knew Padre Pio, Salvatore Pannullo, testified under oath that Padre Pio had received a letter written in Greek—a language unfamiliar to him—but that Padre Pio's Guardian Angel explained the contents to him.

The extraordinary help received from his Guardian Angel assisted Padre Pio in writing in foreign languages as well. This is strong testimony for the angels who encourage all of us to reject the limitations and unnecessary boundaries we impose on our lives. We should not automatically denounce anything that we initially perceive to be "foreign" or "unknown" to our consciousness. One of my favorite inspirational quotes from Padre Pio's writing is, "Don't worry, the Angel of the Lord will go with you."

One time a parishioner of his had a sister who was gravely ill with pneumonia. The woman went to the friary to inform Padre Pio and to seek his help, but the friary was closed. So the woman said to her own Guardian Angel, "Go and tell Padre Pio that I have come for his help, otherwise my sister will die." In a moment she heard Pio's voice inside the church asking, "Who is calling me at this hour? What's wrong?"[3]

The angels are always at your service for healing. In my own sessions with clients I often act as a channel to help make easier the contact with the angels for those in need of healing. During a typical session, I will open with prayer and invite the angels to join me in the healing session through an invocation. I will lay hands on the clients and guide them in meditations to assist them in visualizing their healing. My session will typically close with a prayer of thanks.

During these healing sessions, I have witnessed numerous cases of healing, and they never fail to astonish and delight me. One of my own teachers taught me that as soon as healers no longer experience a feeling of awe in witnessing a healing, they should stop being healers. Of course, it is not I doing the healing. Like the angels, I, too, am only a channel through which God, the Great Physician, sends His healing.

Many of the people who have experienced angelic healing during these sessions describe a feeling like "electricity" surging through their bodies. They mention how the feeling leaves them in a state of vibrant joy, happiness, and well-being long after the session is over. Many other people who have experienced healing even outside of my counseling sessions tell about their tremendous feelings of ecstasy that such angelic collaboration can create and how this strange and wonderful energy runs through their bodies. Also there have been many cases in which people strongly sensed that they were going to get better later.

Others have had ulcers, back pains, and infertility reversed through cooperation with the angels. I have personally seen one case in which a woman, diagnosed with a malignant tumor, received one healing session from the angels and returned to her doctor, only to discover that the tumor had miraculously disappeared. This doesn't happen in every case, of course, but I have no doubt about the willingness or effectiveness of the angels in healing illness.

I witnessed another case in which a client came to me for a session with the healing angels one week before she was scheduled to be operated on for a tumor in her abdomen. The tumor, which was the size of a grapefruit, was causing her great pain. Days after the session, a new battery of blood work and x-rays revealed that surgery would not be necessary as the tumor had disappeared. The doctor could give her no explanation for this.

At the time the healing took place, the woman told me that during the session she felt as if "spiritual hands had removed something" from her physical body and that immediately after the session, the pain that she had previously experienced so intensely had ceased.

Another client had gone for a second set of x-rays for a diagnosed colon tumor. Prior to having the x-rays, however, she came for an angelic healing session. After the x-rays were developed, the technician asked her, "What are we looking for? There's nothing showing in the colon."

Sometimes the healing extends beyond the client's benefit. Recently my father was in the hospital for a routine biopsy to determine if a tumor was cancerous. I had driven my parents to the local hospital early in the morning and had gone on to work. My mother was to call me at work to let me know when to pick them up and take them back home. Not long after I arrived at work the angels told me that something had gone wrong. My father was not going to die, I sensed, but something had happened during the biopsy. Shortly after the angels' message, I received a phone call from my mother informing me that I could pick her up—but that Dad would not be coming with us. He had sustained extensive bleeding from the surgery.

As I drove to the hospital, the angels continued to reassure me that my father was going to be all right. From reading the energy fields of the nurses and doctors—which I am able to do intuitively—I knew that something had indeed gone wrong during the surgery. When I left the hospital with my mother, I asked the healing angels to lovingly watch over my father. I remember driving away feeling very puzzled as to what had actually occurred. A nurse later that evening mentioned in conversation with my father that the needle used in the surgery had a jagged edge and was the cause of the excessive bleeding.

Several days later, to the elation of my entire family, my father was released from the hospital and fully recovered from the surgery. The biopsy revealed that the tumor was non-cancerous. The angels informed me in meditation that day that a healing had actually taken place for my father. Now Dad is back to total wellness and to his daily routine of tending his roses.

I believe that a healing occurred with the doctor and nurses as well. Flower A. Newhouse in her book, *Rediscovering the Angels*, states that the angels "inspire doctors and direct nurses as to how to care for those in their charge."[4] I feel that the experience with my father was an inspiration to the medical staff as well because it helped them to be more careful with their equipment in future surgeries. The help of the angels can touch many lives, when they are called upon through your prayers for others.

In addition to physical healing, I have seen powerful spiritual healing take place through cooperation with the angels. I have seen people who came into a session feeling hostile and hopeless leave almost "floating" out the door, just because they allowed themselves to feel the healing touch of the angels.

I receive letters weekly from individuals who share how the angels have changed their attitude and outlook on life. One individual came to me stating that she was very unhappy and felt that life had cheated her. Her focus, as we began the session, was on how she had never obtained in life what she felt she deserved. She recounted how she had received neither love from her parents nor respect from her spouse. She was having what I call her own private "self-pity party" as she expounded upon what others had not given her. She felt she was getting the short end of the stick at work, in her relationships, and in her life. As a result of her healing session with the angels, however, this woman changed her attitude from being a "go-getter" in life to being a "go-giver." The angels gave her the assignment of seeing how many ways she could give of herself for just the pure joy of giving. She tried it for a month, and miraculously the feeling of being cheated by life dissolved as she discovered how the joy of giving brings blessings into life.

We all can find more satisfaction in life through giving. Just by offering a helping hand to a stranger, showing courtesy to a shopper in a store, or sending someone an uplifting note, you send angelic healing. Just do as the angels do by giving of yourself!

People often share with me how the feeling they received from an angelic healing session stays with them for days. I have seen the ministering angels at work and I have witnessed their limitless power and love in action. People have felt the touch of their hand and known the comfort and assurance of their presence. I have seen clients *loved* back to life spiritually, mentally, emotionally, and physically. While many have not actually seen the faces of the angels, they have allowed themselves to step into their light, love, and illumination for an unmistakable experience.

When I work with the angels in healing sessions, there is no magic or hocus-pocus involved. Nothing weird or bizarre takes place. I simply offer myself as a pipeline of love from heaven and work with the angels in letting God's love and healing power flow to the individual. I must emphasize here that *I myself do not possess the power to heal.*

I compare myself to a Western Union telegram. I am not the words or the message sent by God but merely the modality by which it is sent. The truth is that you can do this, too, in your own life. You don't need a healing counselor, such as myself, to bring healing in your life. What you need is openness, sincerity, and lots of practice.

William Bloom, in his book *Devas, Fairies, and Angels*, shares his belief that there is a large school of angels whose major emphasis is healing. He believes that angel healing is as much a reality in the high-tech hospital intensive care unit as it is in the private office of a spiritual healer.[5] I believe the angels are waiting to assist *all* who ask for healing.

Mr. Bloom encourages people who work in the healing field to use angelic help and to ask for the guidance of healing angels. By asking, the healer will receive an "awareness" from the angels of the best course of healing for the patient. Though not giving specific brand names, Mr. Bloom also states that angels have been involved in the discoveries of many useful antibiotics, anaesthetics, and analgesics.[6]

As I've stated before, healing is yours for the asking from the angels, but I often meet people who do not feel worthy to receive these blessings. They assume that they are not good enough for the angels to be concerned about them. But your self-image has nothing to do with the angels' willingness to help you. In God's eyes you are perfect. That is how you were created. By accepting healing and its possibilities, you are acknowledging this truth as real. The deservedness of your soul is in no way limited by the behavior of your often confused personality. The angels' healing is a gift given freely to you just for believing that you deserve it. And what a gift it is!

When I work with clients, I always have them boldly

decree, right out loud, what it is they want healed. When the person is too weak, as in the case of someone in a hospital, I offer myself as the proxy for the individual in making the decree. You can do this for yourself and for others, too. Help them get their needs out into the open. By decreeing, we are establishing a pattern for thought-substance to reshape whatever is disharmonious into positive, harmonious energy.

With my trained inner vision, I have seen the angels enter the rooms of hospitals and flood their healing light into ill bodies, organs, the very cells of the patients. People have been fortified by the angels, and given strength and courage to overcome even the most severe maladies.

I now have the pleasure of sharing with you the steps I would recommend for working with the healing angels. If you want to open channels of healing for others, have them sit comfortably in a chair while you stand behind them. Begin your healing session with prayer. Open yourself to the angels' healing energies and state your intention to work with them as a channel for God's healing. Release all anxiety as to whether the session will be a success or failure. Let God and the angels work out the details of the session. Above all, let "God's will be done" during the session.

Here is an effective prayer that you can use to open the session. It's all right to read it, until you memorize it or a prayer of your own.

Dear God and Angels of Healing, I offer myself as a channel for healing. Send through me your healing vibration so a "remembrance" of divine origin can occur within (name). Let every cell and molecule of his/her being remember and return to its original state of perfection. Through this healing session, may all that is discordant and disharmonious within the physical, emotional, and mental bodies of (name) be transmuted into light. In God's most holy name, "I AM," we accept this call fulfilled.

Establish a link among yourself, the client, and the angels. One way is to hold the hands of the client or place your hands on their shoulders or head. By doing this, you are establishing a physical connection while the angels establish spiritual contact with you. By this contact, God will be able to send healing through you to the client. Contact is possible from holding their hands because the hands connect to the whole nervous system. By holding the thumb and fingers, a link can be established to any part of the body. When you place your hands on the shoulders, you are near the center of an important group of glands (pituitary, pineal, thyroid) which regulate the entire body. By placing your hands on the head, you are establishing a link with the brain, which has within it a center corresponding to every organ in the body. Your hands become the link, then, through which the angels will scan and examine the body.

Once you establish contact, do not feel that you have to be thinking about what is wrong with the person or how to "fix it." Let God and the angels deal with that in their own way. Open yourself to impressions that the angels may send you. These can be feelings, images, sounds, or words. Each healer is different and can receive messages in different ways. Then, you will have to use wisdom to judge whether the information will be helpful to the person. You may find, for example, that you are given strong impressions as to what emotional or mental cause created the health problem. You can also get a sense of how you should share it, if at all.

Ask the person at this time to decree out loud their request for healing. For example, a client who is experiencing back pain may decree, "I decree here and now for freedom from all pain in my lower back."

You may begin to feel a gentle electric current pulsating through you. If you practice meditation, you will sensitize yourself to this subtle sensation from the angels. You may suddenly feel that another area needs healing, so you may place your hands there and allow the energy to flow to it.

The purpose of the following hand work I will describe is to cleanse the aura and revitalize the nervous center and brain cells. Harmony will be restored to the body by restoring harmony to the higher bodies that surround it. When there is harmony, there is health.

To use this auric massage technique, stand behind the person and gently place your fingers between the client's brow and hairline. Now stroke back with both hands from the forehead toward the ears. Draw your hands rapidly away from the ears in a "clearing away" motion. By these actions you are cleansing the person's aura of any discordant or negative energy and assisting the angels in clearing away the energy of disease in the area. Repeat this movement six or seven times.

Now brush your fingers from the brow back over the top of the head and down to the nape of the neck in the same clearing motion for approximately the same number of times. By going through these moves you are again assisting the angels in clearing away the energy of disease in the aura.

While standing to the side or stooping, place one hand on the solar plexus (just above the diaphragm) and your other hand on the small of the back. Allow the healing energy to flow through your hands. Visualize it. Feel it. *Know* that it is there. This energy will be conveyed to every part of the person's nervous system. Four or five minutes should be sufficient time for this part of the session.

Now, lightly place your hands on the person's head. In a short time you will feel the flow of energy start again. The healing energies are now recharging the brain cells back to their original state of health and vitality. If at any time you feel that you should change or alter the routine because of messages that you are getting from the angels, by all means do so.

As you draw your session to a close, remember to finish just as you began, with prayer. Give thanks for the healing that has been received. Usually I close my sessions by saying: "We give thanks to God and to all His angels of service for all love, support, and healing we received and were witness to here today. May God be glorified by this healing."

Whenever you ask for healing, whether for yourself or for someone else, conclude it with prayers of thanksgiving. This is important because it is your statement of faith that healing has already occurred, and it has.

You can also ask the angels to assist you in healing yourself. I encourage you to try the following exercise when you are experiencing discomfort or pain in any part of your body.

Sit quietly in a chair or lie down on a bed. Breathe in deeply, exhale, and completely relax. Release all anxiety as to whether the healing will be successful because you are both channel and recipient of the energies. Breathe in deeply again, exhale, and feel all tension, doubt, or fear just fall away. Offer a simple opening prayer to God and the angels: "Dear Heavenly Creator and Healing Angels, I open myself to receiving the light and love of God that heals."

Decree out loud your request for healing: "By this healing I am free of this headache (or pain or discomfort)."

Establish a link between yourself and the angels by

visualizing God's healing energy coming from above and flowing through you. You may visualize the energy as white light or sense it as a particular color. However you see the light, visualize the energy flowing through your body to the location of the affected area. It can help if you put your hands over the area. Visualize the energy as it flows through your hands, taking away all disharmony and discordant energies. Allow yourself to feel a continuous current of electricity moving down through the top of your head, into your body, and to the area that is in need of healing. The light vibration is cleansing, purifying, and restoring every cell back to perfect health.

As you receive the healing energies inside your body, visualize an angelic presence standing behind you brushing your aura and clearing away any negative emanations in your energy field. Feel a totality of the angels' healing. Know that you are drawing healing from God through your body, mind, and emotions. Open yourself to the acceptance of God's healing energy that is rejuvenating your body. Whether you feel it or not, know that you received it. With practice, you will no doubt feel the lovely sensation of this healing energy.

Conclude your session with a prayer of thanks for God's healing and for the assistance of the angels in ministering His healing.

As I mentioned, I have seen extraordinary physical healings occur, but more often the healing has been gradual. This is because a deeper healing can take place through the illumination the person gains during his or her experience with the illness. I have actually seen people rejoicing over the wisdom they've gained through an illness. I've seen this manifest as healing not only in their bodies but also in their family life as well. I've also seen how illness has served as the catalyst by which people have discovered the reality of the angels in their lives, and even the love of the Christ.

Through the angels' love and the emergence of the Christ Presence that can manifest during a successful healing session, people have been lifted out of the depths of despair, worry, and illness and been resurrected into the light of God's eternal love, peace, and joy.

The Christ Presence in our lives is the pattern of Jesus within us, the perfect expression of God's love on earth. Through the intercession and invocation of the angels in our physical and spiritual healing, I have seen many people raised closer to that goal than they'd ever been before.

Jesus was able to perform instantaneous healing because He lived at the level of Christ Consciousness where there is no disease. He healed others by God's power working through Him. Perfect health is the will of God— and nowhere is there any record of Jesus refusing to heal someone. God gives each of us the free will to determine how we live our lives. So, as you enter into the desire to help others heal or to heal yourself, hear Jesus gently say to you, "Wilt thou be made whole?" (John 5:6)

When working with clients, I encourage them to use inspirational affirmations such as, "I am one with Christ, who lights my way every day" or "The Son of God in me is saying, 'I am the way, the truth, and the life,'" because Jesus' healing radiation is powerful and the affirmation brings you closer to it. By saying these affirmations with authority, you are stating the authority of Christ within you.

Through Jesus we can experience the realization that holiness and healthiness reflect the state of oneness with God. Nothing is impossible with God. The Creator who formed your body and the love that breathed life into it can restore you, heal you, and make you whole. Accept your healing now. Accept God's love for you. This is the message of the healing angels.

As the story about Margaret at the beginning of this chapter illustrates, healings are often the result of cooperation between members of the angelic realm and members of the medical realm. We must realize that we have incarnated at a time when the brilliance of Western medicine is available to us, and it should not be categorically excluded. Keep in mind also that the exercises in this book are recommended as healing enhancers, and not as substitutes for professional medical care.

It is God's will that you be totally healthy, abundant, and blessed. Those who have sincerely sought the healing energies of the angels have never been left unhealed. Even if the will of God determines that the time isn't right for the body to be free of the illness, the emotional, mental, or spiritual body has most definitely received a full measure of the touch of the healing angels.

Another of the angels' great gifts is to guide us through the transition of death. In my angelic healing work I have been called upon to comfort people who have had family members departing from this realm to the next. I have seen the angels who lead people through their transition, and I've seen the angels who wait to greet these people on the other side. In each case I have witnessed through my inner vision how the deceased were accompanied by their own Guardian Angel, as well as by the angels of service known as the Angels of Transition, sometimes called the Angels of Death.

In every case, even though aware of the family's feeling of loss, I was equally aware of the soul's joy upon being reunited with other loved ones and the realization of the continuity of life. Also, I've seen the joy of the angels who receive them.

As a healer, I have come to realize that it is possible for

a person to be healed without being cured. I have seen people who have died in very weak and depleted states being transformed into radiant images of health at the time of their transition.

One such case is the son of my dear friend, Heidi. Her young son Alex died at the age of four from cancer. Prior to his death, Heidi telephoned me from the hospital asking me if the angels could share any guidance on how much more poor Alex would have to endure. His body had become exceedingly frail and he was enduring a lot of pain, as his bodily functions were breaking down. It was more than his mother or father could bear.

In meditation, the angels showed me an image of Alex playing a game of "catch" with a tall, luminous angel. He had crossed over to the playground of a higher realm and was lovingly looking back to his parents and smiling. I knew, then, that he would be leaving his physical body very soon. I was also shown that as Alex ran over to the angel to play, the angel bent down and scooped him up into its arms. As the angel picked him up, Alex was transformed into a perfect state of health. Then the image of the angel was transformed into the image of Jesus. It was of great comfort to his family to know that Alex was now in Jesus' care and was no longer suffering. In the higher realms of spirit, he was once again the happy, healthy soul he had been prior to his bout with cancer.

At various times I have received messages from the healing angels, advising me of the importance of maintaining an attitude of conscious living and conscious dying. Conscious living means living your life in the eternal now and living that moment to the fullest. Conscious dying is taking responsibility for your death by visualizing where you are going and what you are going to be doing when you get there. Just as we create our own reality here on the earth plane, the images that we carry with us at the time of transition will help create our next reality.

In a tape-recorded program, *Shaping Your Personal Vision for a New World Order*, astrologer Robert "Buz" Kent Myers shared a teaching of the Hopi Indians. When a Hopi warrior was going into battle, the wise grandfathers instructed him to visualize in his mind the eventuality of his death. He was also to envision a pony, a blanket, a bow, and arrows that would be waiting there for him, if death came. The Hopi teaching showed that a warrior should be prepared with what he would need, even in death.[7]

The angels are always ready and willing to assist in healing our lives. So, in honor of these wonderful assistants of the Great Physician and Great Healer, I invite you to experience the following healing meditation:

Guided Healing Meditation

Think for a moment as to what kind of healing you want for yourself. What area of your life is in need of healing? Decree out loud for what you desire:

Lord, I decree here and now by the power of God for the healing of _____ . I dedicate this meditation to healing for myself, for everyone who needs healing, and for the planet Earth.

To prepare for your healing experience simply lie down or sit in a comfortable position. Make certain that your arms, legs, and body are extended in a relaxed position. As you allow yourself to feel relaxed, attune to all the wonderful rhythms of your body. Feel your heart pumping. Feel, as your heart beats, that you are in sync with the larger heart beating in all life.

Feel your breath escape as you exhale, and feel the energy-rich light being inhaled along with the air. With every inhalation and exhalation feel a oneness blending between the world within you and the world outside you. Attune to the oneness of your breath and of your heartbeat. You are one with the heart and breath of God. As you attune to the oneness and blend with the divine source of all life, feel your body slowly and safely begin to lightly float.

You can visualize your body being as light as a fluffy cloud. Just as a cloud floats easily across the sky, you are aware that you are floating easily, higher and higher. You are now higher than the room, higher than the building you are in, higher and higher. You are floating in the sky, and you have no fear as you float, for you are one with all of life. You are one with your body, one with your breath, one with your heart, one with the room, one with the building, one with the sky. You are one with everything.

Feel yourself go even higher and slowly pass into the higher realms of light. You are drawing ever closer to the Divine as you feel yourself surrounded with the bright light and love of the radiant angels. You continue to feel the oneness. You feel electrifying pulsations of energies being sent to you from the angels. You may be aware of the pulsations manifesting as colors, sounds, or visions. Allow yourself to feel the loving energy. Bask in it. Bathe in it. Feel a unity and oneness with the angelic realm and the angels. With their love. Their guidance. Their protection. With their healing.

Trust that whatever healing you needed in your life when you began this meditation is being radiated to you. There is a calmness being radiated to you from the angels. Let the calmness surround you, protect you, and embrace you. Allow yourself to exist in the beautiful energy of the angels' peace.

If you wish, allow yourself to ask the angels to reveal to you how you can solve a particular problem in your daily life. Experience a feeling of joy as you begin to become one with the all-knowing mind of God. Know that an insight is being given to you by the angels and joyously embrace it. The answers that you have been trying to find from outside yourself are now pulsating within you. The angels will tell you if your problems and your illness are related.

Visualize the angels as they place around you a brilliant golden robe that enfolds your entire being. One angel steps forward from the host and invites you to move toward an ornate fountain spraying bright light. As you move forward, you know you are going to receive an irrevocable consecration of your life. You feel your soul dedicated and committed to becoming one with the will of God so that your highest plan may be realized in your life.

You are preparing to dedicate yourself and your life to your highest good. The angel dips its hand into the fountain and blesses your hands—first the left, then the right—and charges you with the will of God, so all that you reach for and use your hands for will be for your highest good.

The angel again dips its hand into the fountain and blesses your feet with the light so that your feet are charged with the will of God. Your feet will now lead you to your highest good. The angel blesses your lips so that you will speak only the truth as you know it. It blesses your ears so that you will hear only the music of the spheres, the sound of harmony in your life and in the world around you. The angel blesses your eyes so that you will see only the divinity in all life and only good for yourself and others. It blesses the top of your head, consecrating your wonderful mind so that your thoughts will be inspirational and clear.

Placing its hands upon your shoulders, the angel gently whispers in your ear, "Claim your wings and *fly*, beloved! Release all the old patterns and thought forms that hold you back. Release your illness and fly toward your highest good!" Allow yourself to feel the joy and exhilaration of this moment for as long as you like, and savor it with your senses.

In gratitude for this sacred moment, offer the following prayer to the healing angels:

Dear Healing Angels,
    As I sit here faith-filled, I can feel your healing love flow through every cell of my body, making it whole, vibrant, and alive. I thank you, angels, for your healing presence within me. Your healing love has touched me and blessed me. My spirit is radiant and free! I will unfurl my wings and fly to total fulfillment, total perfection, and total healing. Thank you, thank you, thank you!

✢ ✢ ✢

When you are ready, return to your physical body and to the room, this space, this moment. Remember in all that you do to let your thoughts, words, and actions assist you in claiming your wings and flying to your highest good. May the fulfillment of your highest good be a healing in the lives of others.

·CRIS ARBO·

Chapter Seven

Honor the Angelic Presence in All Life

*"For thou hast made him a little lower than the angels,
and hast crowned him with glory and honour."*
Psalm 8:5

Anyone who has experienced the angels firsthand knows the thrill of what their unique light energy is like. It's a special, subtle, exhilarating sensation that makes you feel secure, happy, and loved inside. But angelic light energy also has a way of helping you experience the oneness of all life—and that you are an important part of that oneness.

It works the other way, too. The closer you become to the angels by actually looking for the light of oneness in life, the closer will you draw to the angelic kingdom.

It works like a magnet.

Every time you pause to observe a gentle rain, see the sun shining through the drops, or appreciate God's light show when a magnificent rainbow spreads across the sky, know that these gentle observances honor the divinity in all creation.

As I've mentioned before, divine energy is stepped down to our level of perception through the angelic kingdom, so when I see little white snowbells bursting forth from the tree at winter's end or a robin hopping across my yard in the early spring, I know the angels are helping me to see messages of God's presence in all life. I can hear them whispering to me, "God is here, God is there, and God is everywhere."

I have heard some people say with confidence that this is their last incarnation on earth; or others say that they can't wait to be finished with this "cycle of necessity." But I have difficulty thinking about leaving this plane. There's beauty all year round, if you look for it. When everything turns green and the daffodils appear like trumpets heralding the spring; or in summer, when gardens overflow with an abundance of juicy vegetables; or in the fall, when the leaves on the trees change to crimson, yellow, and orange; or in winter, when ice crystals coat the trees—leaving the earth is the farthest thing from my mind!

The angels encourage us to take time to honor the divinity, the light of God, in all life and in all seasons. As I said above, taking time to appreciate life—every leaf, every blade of grass, and every flower—to love all the animals and the plants, and especially human life will bring you closer to the angels and, therefore, closer to God. God is in all of us, in all places, in all things. God is all.

Consuella Newton, a teacher and lecturer in the field of higher consciousness and the originator of the Integrated

Awareness Technique, by which you can learn to develop your intuition, is also the creator of a powerful affirmation which I often use. It reads as follows:

"I am the Light. The Light is within me. The Light moves throughout me. The Light surrounds me. The Light protects me. I AM THE LIGHT."

Many religions of the world promote the idea that we are one with everything around us. The beauty of the world, when we choose to see it, is a reflection to us that we, too, are beautiful. The angels try to remind us to honor the light in all life every day and to appreciate our own life and light so that we never forget.

One time of day that is especially desirable for honoring the divinity in all life is the evening, during which you set aside time for prayer. If there is one thing I feel we have lost in our revolutionary modern ways, it is an appreciation for the evening hours. Those of you with children, I encourage you to make evenings special in your household. In the rhythmic pattern of the day, it is a perfect time to slow down and honor the hard work, joys, and blessings of life.

The Bible reiterates the message that we do not rest in order to be able to do more work, but rather that we labor in order to enter a time of rest: "There remaineth therefore a rest to the people of God. For he that is entered into his rest, he also hath ceased from his own works, as God did from his. Let us labour therefore to enter into that rest . . . " (Hebrews 4:9-11)

It is my belief that the rest described in Genesis after the creation of the universe was really the opportunity for God to commune with all life that He had created. When we follow His example and take time to rest in our lives, we, too, commune with the divine presence in all life, including our own.

Another way to honor the oneness in all life is to make yourself enthusiastic about living. The word *enthusiasm* comes from the Greek "en theos" which means "in God." When you lack enthusiasm in your life, you are not living your life "in God"; that is, you are not honoring God's presence in your thoughts, actions, words, and deeds. Be excited about life, and you will see conditions change dramatically. If you have lacked enthusiasm in the past, learn now to cultivate it. Here are some ideas that can help you achieve unbounded, vibrant enthusiasm in your life.

When you awake in the morning, do an "angelic accounting" of your life; that is, count up all the good you have every day and the most recent blessings that have come into your life. Henry David Thoreau, the American philosopher, would lie in bed for a while each morning reminding himself of all the good in his life: that he had a healthy body, that his mind was alert, his work interesting. The more "angelic accounting" you do, the more good you'll discover for which you can account.

Do an "angelic cleaning" of your mind. Thoughts are things that occupy space in your mental field. It is widely believed today that a great majority of bodily ills have been induced by negative thoughts with which we have poisoned our minds. We do this with worry about our jobs, our lack of prosperity, our health, and our loved ones. Prolonged periods of worry, anger, tension, fear, and resentment actually invite physical illness. On the other hand, a healthy state of mind is achieved and maintained when you willingly let go of stress and fear, and allow the space to be filled with positive thoughts. Empty your mind of any negative or depressing thoughts.

It's important to review your day and think about any mistakes you may have made. Draw all the lessons you can from them, solve what can be solved, and then release them. Worry and depressive mental ruts can only serve to keep you down and thoroughly unenthusiastic.

There is one day a year that is a perfect opportunity to engender enthusiasm and honor the oneness in your life. It is a day that is also celebrated in the angelic kingdom, though you wouldn't ordinarily think so. That day is your birthday!

Your birthday is a very special day, whether you honor it or not. It is the day on which your spirit came into embodiment on the earth plane. To me, birthdays are sacred days. I encourage people to celebrate the day by doing something that reflects the energy they want to manifest in the year ahead. Instead of dwelling on gifts or dreading one's age, try to see every birthday as a new beginning. Let it be one of the holiest days in your personal year.

On this day the angels shower us with an outpouring of spiritual illumination, with which we may or may not choose to connect. The angels give us the blessing that, in the year to come, we will find an abundance of opportunities to realize our highest good.

There is another day each year that is special among the angels. On September 30, a joyous holy day is celebrated in the angelic realm on behalf of the people on earth. It is called the Angels Harvest Day, and it is similar to Thanksgiving Day. On Thanksgiving Day, Americans take time to give thanks for the abundant harvest of blessings in their lives. On Angels Harvest Day, the angelic host reports on the progress or "harvest" of the efforts of the angels to be of help on earth. After the report is given, in the form of an exchange of Heavenly Consciousness, God determines what additional resources need to be made available to the angels to help facilitate their work here.

During the Angelic Harvest ceremony, all the angels

who minister to the earth offer as a sacrifice to God the light of their wonderful work and service for the year that has just passed.

Because of their mass request—an awesome expression of love that I have witnessed in meditation—God grants these selfless servants additional light for their use in the upcoming year. As reported in the September 1990 issue of *Take Charge of Your Life* magazine, at the Angelic Harvest held in 1987, a divine ceremony took place during which the angels were granted dispensation to raise humanity into a higher consciousness in evolution.[1] The additional qualities of God which were brought into the earth's atmosphere at that time are assisting in the spiritual awakening now occurring on the planet. As I shared with you in Chapter Two, there are at this time twelve Archangels and twelve Archaii working with humanity. As a result of this dispensation, they are now fully projecting the emanations of the twelvefold energy of God to earth. Many people who have sensitized themselves to the higher vibrations have been able to feel it.

Not only do I like to look for the angelic presence in all life, I like to look for angels everywhere I go. You can join me in being on this "angel alert." Angels are everywhere, reflecting the message of our oneness with God. You can see the light of the angels when you pause to gaze upon a candle or when you fix your sight upon a star. The oneness is reflected back to you, as the shining light reminds you to let your light shine, too. You can see the love of the angels when you gaze into the eyes of a friend, a lover, or a pet. The oneness is reflected back to you by the warmth you feel, reminding you to share your warmth, too.

Where else can you see the angelic presence at work on the earth? Look at the clouds, the waters, the flames, and the very stones themselves.

As we discussed in Chapter Two, the intelligences that govern the elements of air, fire, earth, and water are also a part of the angelic kingdom. But did you know that these Elementals eventually evolve to the status of "angel"? Geoffrey Hodson states that, "Angels have risen (through evolution) from the nature-spirits of earth."[2]

I love watching the work of the Elementals. I, and many others, can see them in the woods, in the flames, and in the water. Awareness of the Elementals will enhance your ability to see the angelic presence in all life.

In the clouds I love watching these aspiring angels playing. I call it "angel art." When I see the clouds taking on formations in the sky, I know the angels are at work, being artistic with the assistance of the air Elementals. I think the angels are doing trial runs of tasks they have been given to perform, so the sky becomes a drawing board for them. I have also seen the Elementals in fire. I'd like to recount a personal experience that beautifully illustrates the work of these fire Elementals as well as cooperation among the kingdoms.

I had taken a class with Phoebe Reeves, a woman who teaches about the alliance that exists among all kingdoms. During that class Phoebe showed us a video on firewalking. I knew nothing of firewalking up to the moment I viewed the video, but I knew as I watched that some day I was going to walk on fire. Firewalks have become more popular in recent years as a way in which participants can push through their fears and walls of limitation. Through faith alone, individuals actually walk unharmed across a bed of burning embers. I just knew that this was for me. After Phoebe's class I immediately signed up for her next firewalk workshop.

On the evening prior to the scheduled firewalk, however, I received a phone call advising me that there weren't enough people to hold the workshop. I was disappointed and somewhat confused as I just *knew* that I was supposed to walk on fire. I let it go, trusting that there was a higher plan involved.

Within a month's time Phoebe called me and asked if I would consider staging a firewalk on my property. I enthusiastically agreed. I finally was going to be able to walk on fire and it would be on my beloved land. Many of my friends signed up for the workshop, but none were as certain as I that there was nothing to firewalking. I felt that the experience would be natural for me. So when I heard someone comment about the possibility of getting burnt, I wouldn't give it an ounce of energy. Nothing was going to stop me from walking on fire.

On the evening of the firewalk the logs were stacked and ignited. We sang songs and said prayers, but as I stood in the heat of the burning logs and heard Phoebe describe how the raked-out coals would be 2,000 degrees, a little voice suddenly began to question my desire to take this little walk. I heard the voice say, "Maybe you'll walk on fire in this life—but not necessarily tonight." Then the coals were raked out and against the darkness of the night they sparkled like shimmering orange diamonds. Then I watched in awe as Phoebe gracefully danced on the fire.

We had all been instructed to listen to our own inner wisdom for guidance as to whether or not we were to take the firewalk that night. I was trying to listen for my angels, but that little voice in my head kept interjecting its two cents. To add even more confusion to my decision, one of my best friends suddenly got her inner message loud and clear to GO!— and she was the first of our group to dash across the coals.

So there I stood before the fire, wondering now if I was doing it for me or feeling pressure because she had done it.

I was also wondering where my conviction for firewalking disappeared after I had had it for the last two months. I just looked and stared into the fire, praying for guidance from the angels as to if and when I should walk. Then as I gazed into the glowing coals, I was suddenly able to "see" the fire Elementals smiling at me as they, too, danced among the flames. They spoke to me and in my mind I heard these words:

"Do you love us?"

I replied, "Why, of course, I do!"

They answered back, "And we love you, Janie."

Then they asked, "Do you respect and honor us?"

Again, I stated, "I most certainly do!"

And they responded, "And we respect and honor you, too, Janie."

Then they got to the real issue by asking, "Do you know that we have the potential to burn you?"

I answered back, "Yes, you'd better believe I do!"

Before I could say anything more, they added, "That is all it is—the *potential* to burn you. You are the one who gives power to the potential. We cannot burn you unless you give us the power to burn you."

As I listened, I suddenly began to feel the excitement grow once again in my heart. The dear little fire Elementals opened a path to me across the coals. Mind you, it was a very *direct* path that got me across the fire quickly, but they showed me the way to claim my own power and to make my run to victory.

That was an evening I will treasure always, and I will never forget the wonderful lesson taught to me by the precious fire Elementals of the angelic kingdom. We must honor the angelic presence in all life—even in fire. I have participated in firewalks on numerous occasions since that first evening. Each walk is a different experience because life is always changing. There is life in the fire, in the participants, and in the ritual of the walk itself. No two firewalks are ever the same because no two moments are the same and our consciousness is ever changing.

The fire Elementals are present in physical fire, but they also exist in spiritual fires. There is a special spiritual flame that corresponds to each of the twelve rays and we can use these flames as tools in our visualizations. (See Figure 2.2.) When you picture a ray's color in the form of a flame, you can use it in your meditations and prayers. For example, you can use blue fire in your visualizations for developing your faith and courage, and pink fire for developing love.

One of the greatest gifts being brought to the earth in this new Aquarian age is the violet fire. It is the rich violet color in an African violet blossom or in the heart of an amethyst crystal. You can use it to help manifest freedom and forgiveness in your life and for transmuting karma. The violet fire can help you see the angelic presence in all life by clearing and purifying your perceptions.

For those who have never heard of these "invisible" fires, there are several references to them in the Bible. When John said that Jesus " . . . shall baptize you with the Holy Ghost, and with fire," (Matthew 3:11) he wasn't referring to physical fire but to spiritual fire. So was Jesus when He said, "I am come to send fire on the earth; and what will I, if it be already kindled?" (Luke 12:49) Some believe that the gift of violet fire is one of the true meanings of these quotes. Edgar Cayce also spoke of the use of the "violet ray" applicator in several of his health-related psychic readings.

The violet fire cleanses and purifies, dissolving any negativity we put into that flame. In addition to possessing the gift of violet fire, each of us has access to a violet fire angel. Violet fire angels have volunteered to assist every man, woman, and child on earth to transmute negative energy in their lives.

All you need to do in order to work with the violet fire and with your personal violet fire angel is to focus on this selfless friend right in your own energy field. Simply ask the angel for help in transmuting that which you want changed in your life. Offer yourself as a vehicle for God's gift of the violet fire energy. It will be sent to you by your violet fire angel in an etheric liquid form. Visualize it as it enters through the top of your head and fills and lights each part of your body.

Visualize your angel taking a pitcher and pouring this violet liquid elixir into your being. The violet energy will flow into all your organs, bones, blood, and skin and will completely saturate all the cells of your body. Visualize yourself being transformed into a large violet flame. As you visualize this, know that you are becoming one with God. Expand even farther and see your flame become a sun so that you are now radiating and projecting the light of the violet fire to others.

Another way to flood your being with violet fire during the day is to visualize the violet fire energy glowing in each glass of water that you drink. As you drink, ask the violet fire angel working with you to utilize the energy to transmute any discordant vibration within your being. Using the violet fire, you will in time come to realize an increased sense of well-being and a much more profound sense of the angelic presence in all life and your oneness with it.

Another experience I had which helped me to honor the angelic presence in all life actually took place amid the realm of the earth Elementals. Further, it helped me realize how our oneness with the universe transcends death. At the time I was taking part in a vision quest ritual, again on my property. A vision quest is a Native American ceremony during which an individual spends time alone with nature seeking "vision" or insight into his or her life. During the "quest," meditation, prayer, and rituals are often used to expand the experience.

In our vision quest workshop, participants individually selected a certain focus to work on as well as an area in the woods where they would spend the next twenty-four hours meditating and anticipating possible spiritual visions that would come forth. For my specific focus I chose the little pet cemetery where my precious animals were buried. One of the goals for this quest was to transcend our boundaries. For some the boundary was the fear of being alone in the dark. For others it was the boundary of confronting the elements, as it was rainy and cold that night. As for me, I wanted to transcend the boundary of grief I'd experienced from the loss of my animal friends to death.

Armed with only my sleeping bag, I claimed my spot in the woods and began my quest. I had the advantage of being familiar with the woods, since it was my home; however, when darkness settled around me, compounded with a driving rain that soaked me to the bone, all familiarity dissipated and I began to wonder how anything inspirational could come from this experience. I prayed to God that the twenty-four hours would pass quickly. I prayed for warmth. I prayed to be dry. I prayed that in the future I would never sign up for another vision quest!

These initial requests came from my ego personality, which was having a fit about being cold, wet, scared, and alone. Slowly, however, an energy of oneness came over me. Even though I was drenched in my sleeping bag, I felt this oneness with the drops of rain falling on the trees and with the wet leaves upon which I was sitting. I felt a oneness with the trees that shared the woods with me, and with the earth Elementals in the ground and stones around me. I felt one with the water Elementals that were purifying my body and the body of the earth.

During that night, the angels gave me a vision of one of my little bunnies, who was buried in the cemetery. He came up to me and nuzzled next to me. It was my sorely missed lop-eared bunny Biloxi. The angels said to me that love is the energy that unites us with all kingdoms, and that love never dies. They told me that whenever I feel loss for my animals I should redirect my energy from focusing on the loss to focusing on the love I felt, because the energy of that love never dies. Love is eternal, after all, and God is love. The angels gave me a valuable gift that evening—the "vision" of how to honor the eternalness of life and love.

One of my favorite summertime relaxations is floating in an inner tube on my parents' country pond. I love the perspective that being in the water gives me. It allows me to float close to the ducks who live on the pond and to the grassy bank, where I can study the wildflowers in bloom. It is always a refreshing experience—physically, mentally, and spiritually.

One particular Sunday afternoon I was lazily drifting in the water. The water was so soothing that I felt as if my body had blended with it and that we had become one energy. I was thinking to myself how much I *loved* the water, when I became aware of the water Elementals speaking to me. They said: "Sister of the human kingdom, we, as you, are expressions of the love of God. When you allow yourself to blend with our vibration, our common love is multiplied in energy and the result is a heightened experience of oneness." That expressed exactly what I was feeling that day, and I never forgot it.

In my work with the angels, they have guided me in the development of a meditation during which the participant visually creates an angelic banner, a personalized symbol that helps you visualize and focus your life with angel consciousness. It's your personal life seal, a flag that flies majestically over your life. I would like to share this meditation with you. As you read these words, consider that you are creating a flag for the nation which is *you*.

Angelic Banner Meditation

Become quiet and relaxed. Ask the angels to join you. Breathing slowly and rhythmically, allow your thoughts to focus on the creation of your flag or banner. Go within your heart and experience a feeling of oneness with God and with all life. Ask your angels to bring into focus before you the components of your personal angelic banner. Let the design come from the wisdom of your soul. Decide first what color background you would like for the banner. See that color. In your mind's eye see the color and fabric of your banner stretched out before you.

Now allow your focus to move to what you'll put in the four corners of the banner. Become aware of objects, figures, or symbols that come to mind as you think about what you "see" there. Perhaps they are items you collect; perhaps they are religious symbols that are important to you. Let the images flow over you. One image for the upper right . . . one for the lower right . . . one for the upper left . . . and one for the lower left. If you see a flower, allow yourself to focus in on what kind of flower. If at first you do not visualize any images, allow your imagination to come into play. Think of any symbols that you want as part of your angelic banner.

Now focus on the center of the banner. Let yourself connect with the heart energy of your flag and allow an image to appear. Remember, you are participating in the creation of a powerful spiritual tool for yourself. Observe your angelic banner and how it reflects messages to you. What symbol will reflect your gifts and talents? How should your ideals be reflected? Your life's bliss? How could you symbolize the eternal energy of love? Don't feel any anxiety over whether or not you receive answers to these questions at this time. Just allow them to lovingly enter your thoughts and know that each time you think about the banner, you will gain additional insight about its meaning.

Now reach higher into the octaves of the angelic realm and ask your angels to reveal to you a motto for your life. It can be a few words or a saying or a slogan. Listen for your life's motto. When you sense a completion of your angelic banner and motto, allow your consciousness to return to the room. Remember to thank the angels for any insights you have received. Immediately write down what you saw and heard during this meditation.

✣ ✣ ✣

Many of my clients go on to physically create their banner either in paper or cloth and hang it in their homes. One woman made a beautiful Native American-style shield containing the visions that appeared on the screen of her mind.

When we honor the divinity in all life, we live in harmony with all of God's creations. We know that all is right with the world. Harmony brings acceptance and tolerance for others. We are not threatened or afraid, for we allow ourselves to be true to our expression of the God within us and allow others to do the same.

Dionysius beautifully summarized it when he wrote about God's goodness shining upon all life and the importance of our being accepting: "For just as the Goodness established by God above all things reaches from the highest and most perfect beings to the lowest . . . It gives light to all that can receive It and creates them and gives them life . . . And if anything does not participate . . . this is not because of any weakness or deficiency in Its distribution of light, but rather is due to an inaptitude for the reception of the light on the part of those things which do not open themselves to receive it."[3]

This is the message of the angels: Accept Now God's Eternal Love—accept your birthright to undivided goodness. Honor the goodness shining in your life by taking care of yourself. The angels encourage us to "lighten up." One of the easiest ways of doing this is to maintain an energy of simplicity in everything we do.

Ours is a world filled with excesses, so the angels invite us to "lighten" the load and make things simpler. We are then able to perceive the oneness of life much easier. Some ways in which you can simplify your life are: Maintain a regular, uncomplicated exercise routine. Develop simple, nutritious eating habits. Keep your life's commitments simple. Do not overextend yourself in any area of your life. Take time to enjoy the ordinary pleasures of life, such as the beauty of sunrises and sunsets. Take time to simply be quiet. Smile often and don't forget to laugh.

As long as you have to *be* something, simply be kind. The Dalai Lama of Tibet has often described his personal religion as just *being kind*. These are only a few of the ways in which you can keep your life simple and bless the angelic presence in all life.

In honor of the angelic presence in your life, I offer the following closing exercise to this chapter as an opportunity for you to experience the light of God that shines within you.

"I Am One with the Light of God" Exercise

To begin, sit comfortably in a chair with your arms and legs uncrossed and your spine as straight as possible. Breathe in deeply. As you exhale, completely relax. Enter meditation and envelop yourself, through visualization, in a powerful force field of white light. This force field will prevent anything that is not of the light from interfering with your sacred activity of meditation.

Once in meditation, see an ornate golden throne. An angelic being beckons you to sit upon it. With every breath you are breathing in this bright light. As your body fills with this light, visualize it as a pure bright, rich gold. See yourself transformed into a light being. Your lungs, your arms, your feet, your body are all filled with the light. You are suddenly weightless. The light expands within your being. As you let your breath out slowly, see the light going forth from you and filling the space around you with pure deep gold light. The light expands farther around you. As you gently inhale and exhale the golden light, decree the following:

"I am awakening to the truth that God is shining in me always. I am one with all life and with all the angelic presence. God shines in me through intelligence and wisdom. I open my mind to God's radiant light and all my thoughts of doubt, darkness, and negativity dissolve. My thoughts are transformed into creativity, imagination, and positive thinking.

"God shines in me as divine love. I open my heart to God's infinite love and all feelings of fear, hate, and resentment vanish. I am filled with thoughts of forgiveness, kindness, and compassion.

"God shines in my body and all tension, stress, disease, and disharmony are transmuted into energy, strength,

and vibrant health. I am whole, strong, and as free as
God created me to be.

"God shines in all my affairs and activities. My life is in
divine order. All illusion of lack, injustice, and imbalance
is replaced by abundance, harmony, justice, and joy.

"God shines through my mind, my heart, my body, and
my life. I, too, am a shining one, because I am one with the
light of God."

Now, gently return your consciousness to the room and
to your present surroundings. Experience the buoyancy
and lightness you are feeling—the oneness you share with
all life and the angelic presence everywhere.

·CRIS ARBO·

Chapter 8

Attune to the Angels

*"Hereafter ye shall see heaven open, and the angels of
God ascending and descending upon the Son of man."*
John 1:51

We live in a world where communications technology
bombards us with all sorts of information at lightning
speed. Fortunately, a vast array of spiritual information is
included in this bombardment, and I believe it's helping a
spiritual awakening to take place on the earth. The more
that people are able to learn about spiritual matters, the
more they want to know. Because of this quest for knowledge, people are changing the way they think about themselves and their spiritual lives.

In my work I have observed how many of my clients are
shifting toward a new consciousness in which they personally claim the reality of their oneness with God. It is my

belief that as the consciousness of more and more people is transformed to embrace this truth, a shift will occur in the energy field of the earth itself. What is happening, as we live and breathe, is the birth of a new golden age of love and spiritual awareness, with the angels playing a key role in its establishment.

To aid us at this time of revelation and transformation, our angelic guardians and spirit guides are cooperating with us to develop and manifest special energy techniques that, though they may not be new in the higher spiritual realms, are indeed new on earth.

The Biblical verse above (John 1:51) refers to "angels of God ascending and descending upon the Son of man." This verse depicts a powerful image of how we, the sons and daughters of God, receive divine energies from higher realms, especially the angelic realm. As we work with these energies in our lives and our consciousness, we can discover a turning point wherein we become one with the spiraling energies that are both "ascending and descending." In short, we can directly access assistance from God through the angels.

One of the greatest blessings in my work with the angelic kingdom has been the discovery of a technique that helps this turning point to manifest. I call it an "Angelic Attunement."

An Angelic Attunement is a special activity of the heavenly host of the utmost significance. It is a technique usually performed by another but which you can perform for yourself, in which you experience a dramatic inpouring of the energies and blessings of the angelic realm. It's quite a remarkable transforming experience for anyone fortunate enough to experience it.

An Angelic Attunement is a blissful transformation and healing experience during which the angels radiate to you a powerful feeling of peace, harmony, love, and oneness with God. Through an Angelic Attunement, you are able to transcend your human level of consciousness and actually communicate telepathically with the angels. The experience also helps you maintain a synchronicity of vibration with them and a feeling of oneness with love, the energy force that operates in all life.

The gift of Angelic Attunements has been given to planet earth to assist people in transforming their lives through dramatic changes in their attitudes and the ways in which they live. The experience itself lasts from several seconds to several minutes, establishing direct "communion"—in the strictest sense of the word—with the angels. Its effect lasts as long as you can maintain your focus—and as long as you don't counter its effect by returning to negative thinking and forgetting your place in God's heart.

Anyone who is acquainted with the angels can receive the assistance of an Angelic Attunement. As long as you believe in the angels as ministering spirits of God, then you can open yourself to receiving this Attunement. It is accomplished in a balanced co-mingling of the angels' willingness and ability to raise everyone closer to God, with the individual's belief in angelic energy, facility with the powers of visualization, clearness of thought, and the following prerequisites. (I will share with you later in the chapter an actual procedure that's based on the Attunements I conduct but which you can use for your own experience.)

Though they are usually done with a conductor such as myself, anyone who desires to work with the Attunement energy can do so.

The first step is desiring the attunement. When you want to attune with the angels, you need not worry about the angelic realm or how to get there. The song, "Never, Never Land" from the musical *Peter Pan*, expresses it best: that it is not on any chart—you find it in your heart. This is what finding the angelic kingdom through an Attunement is like.

The next requirement is knowing precisely what it is that you want to manifest in your life. This is necessary in order for the magnetic power created during an Attunement to be targeted toward some specific goal. It is as if the energy needs a target to lock into before it can begin building a vortex. So before you attempt your Attunement exercise, think about what it is you want to manifest. Remember that because the angels are working toward your highest good and the highest good of all God's creation, the goals you select must be honorable ones. Remember also that there is no such thing as an unrealistic goal.

The main criterion is that your goal be for the highest good of all concerned, as your Attunement is to be a linking with the oneness of all life. Understand that you can have whatever it is you desire, but first you must release all sense of limitation as you enter into your Angelic Attunement.

Pause for a moment and think about your life. What is it that you really want? In order to help you determine this, ask yourself these questions—and don't be afraid to write down your answers for future reference:

What do I want spiritually? Do I want to be closer to God? Do I want to experience a relationship with the angels?

What do I want mentally? Do I want to learn something new? Use more of my mind?

What do I want emotionally? Is there an emotion that always gets the better of me that I would like to diffuse?

What I do want physically? Do I wish to have more energy? Healing of some particular ailment?

What do I want financially? Would I like to be making more money? What would I do with that additional money?

What do I want career-wise? Am I happy in my present job? Am I happy where I work?

What do I want socially? Would I like a rewarding new relationship? Am I looking for new friends?

The idea is to look closely at every area of your life and ask yourself what goals you would like to set for yourself. Once you have determined what it is you want to manifest in your life, state it out loud in the form of a decree. For example:

"Beloved Presence of God 'I AM' in me, I decree that I AM deserving of a fulfilling relationship in my life."

Once you have decided what it is you want and have decreed for it by utilizing the power of words, you are almost ready to proceed with your Angelic Attunement. Remember that once you express the desire to visit the angels through an Attunement exercise and clearly identify what you desire, you will be assisted by them in raising your consciousness high enough in order for the Attunement to take place.

The Attunement energy will help you visualize your life's goal and direct your most positive thoughts to achieving it. So it's important that you have this clearly in mind. This goal or "ideal" that you set for yourself is explained by Cayce in one of his psychic readings: "Then as the guardian influence or angel is ever before the face of the Father, through same may that influence ever speak—but only by the command of or attunement to that which is thy ideal." (1646-1)

Another factor that will help your Attunement be successful is purifying your aura. For these purposes, simply desiring to be one with the vibration of the angels can help neutralize the negative energies around you and in your aura. It works similarly to your basic meditation and healing sessions. However, the difference is that in an Angelic Attunement such purification of the aura increases in manifestation once you and the angels start the energy flowing. It is like a positive domino effect.

Through an Angelic Attunement you experience the sense or revelation that you are love, you are truth, and you are light. The transformational vibration from the realms of celestial angelic light aligns you, so you can move forward with clarity and vision toward what you desire for yourself. In earthly terms, I like to think that the angels give you a "tune-up," an Angelic At-"tune"-ment.

When you express your desire to improve your life through such an experience, the members of the angelic kingdom who can assist you in your growth are automatically drawn to you. They are drawn to you even now, as you read this.

William Bloom explains it as follows: " . . . devas of spiritual growth will begin to be attracted . . . They work in the atmosphere around the individual helping to keep it clean and magnetically pure . . . and keep the atmosphere spiritually playful and sympathetically helpful to the individual."[1]

What makes an Angelic Attunement so unique is how the energy affects you at hidden levels, actually helping to unify and align your subtle bodies. The angels integrate the activities of the seven components of your being during the Angelic Attunement process. (See Figure 8.1.) The result is that God is then better able to manifest His oneness through you continuously on physical, mental, emotional, and spiritual levels. The reason is that you are less in His way!

An Angelic Attunement is, in fact, a seven-level process that aligns the seven components of body, mind, and spirit: the physical, etheric, and astral bodies; the conscious, subconscious, and superconscious elements of your mind; and your spirit or soul.

The physical body is the component with which we are most familiar. This body is merely a three-dimensional representation of the higher "invisible" bodies. It's the physical body that does all the action in the physical world.

We are in the midst of transformational times on this planet. The changes we are experiencing, such as a feeling that time is passing quickly, are both wonderful and somewhat frightening at the same time. Stuart Wilde refers to the speeding up of energy as "the quickening."[2]

Many people feel that time is speeding up, whereas actually our vibrations—you, I, and everything around us—are quickening or moving faster and higher in vibration. As a result of this increased vibration, we are experiencing changes in our physical bodies as we adapt. Perhaps you have noticed some changes in your own consciousness. Take a moment and answer for yourself the following questions:

Have you recently noticed that you have been able to remember more and more about your dreams? Have you noticed that you have become more emotional lately, especially feeling depressed, despondent, or just "wiped out"? Have you noticed that you sometimes wake up between two and four o'clock in the morning feeling refreshed and ready to start your day, but since it is not time for you to get up, you go back to sleep?

Have you been feeling a pulsation or an energy around your forehead that you hadn't noticed before? Have you noticed a quickening energy around your heart, as if you were having palpitations?

The Seven Components
of Body, Mind, and Spirit

<u>Spirit</u>
Soul

<u>Body</u>
Physical Body
Etheric Body
Astral Body

<u>Mind</u>
Conscious
Subconscious
Superconscious

Figure 8.1

An Angelic Attunement aligns the seven components,
helping to break down barriers to realizing our oneness
with God.

If you answered "yes" to a majority of the above questions, these may be signs that you are becoming inwardly aware of these planetary and spiritual changes.

These changes are generally experienced in the physical body, which is also that part of us where disease manifests. This emphasizes the importance of harmonizing the relationship between the physical and etheric bodies. The angels understand this relationship. It is one of the main reasons why Angelic Attunements are beneficial.

The physical body is a carbon copy of the etheric body, which provides the intelligence that builds and maintains the physical organs and tissue. The etheric body provides a balancing function in the physical body. If you lose a limb, the etheric field that surrounded that physical structure takes a while to dissipate. This has been experienced as "phantom pain" by amputation victims who still "feel" the sensation of a limb that no longer physically exists.

During this time of change, we see a greater awareness in the relationship of health and harmony between the etheric and physical bodies. People are becoming more aware that disease can be best understood as "dis-ease," caused by a disharmony or lack of ease in their emotional or mental make-up. Such disharmony in the emotional and mental bodies, therefore, actually results in illness in the physical.

The etheric body appears as the "aura" to those who can see it. Providing healing to one's aura has a positive effect on the physical body because the etheric body is a duplicate of the physical and its influence is dynamic. At the time of death the physical body becomes inoperative and dies. The etheric body also dies, in most cases dissipating within three days. The energy of the etheric field is never lost, however; it merely returns to the source.

The third component is the astral body, which contains

our emotions. This body is sometimes called the "mental body," but it should not be confused with the three components of the mind which I will describe below.

Everything that makes up the astral body when you are living in the physical dimension continues to exist after death and influences the soul. The astral body contains our memory banks and emotional feedback.

The cosmic law of attraction is expertly outlined in Patricia Diane Cota-Robles' book, *The Next Step*. According to this law, as the light of God comes into our bodies, it connects with whatever vibrations are in our consciousness. The synthesis of these vibrating energies is projected into physical form and thereby manifests in our lives. As Cota-Robles states, "Everything manifests in our lives now, whether we are referring to our financial situation, health, relationships, careers, happiness, success or peace of mind, is a result of our beliefs, thoughts, words, actions, and feelings."[3] The emotions that dominate our astral body are those that shape our reality in the next world. Angelic Attunements help align the emotions and thoughts with the physical body to make sure the predominant energy is beneficial and positive throughout the life and beyond.

Many of us have experienced the sensation of traveling within our astral bodies, especially during dream or sleep experiences. You may have awakened during the night, bathed in perspiration, having the feeling that your body has just "dropped" into bed after being far away. Sometimes the "drop" actually jolts you awake. Such an experience is often referred to as an "out-of-body" experience; when the truth of the matter is that you slipped from your physical to astral body and back again for a dream journey. More and more people are sensing the existence of their astral body during mystical experiences or in a life-threatening situation.

The next three components are elements of the mind. The conscious mind is associated with ego and the mundane world, though it's only ten percent of your total consciousness. Many people get caught up in the illusions created by the conscious mind when it is used as a puppet of the ego.

Yet we are all aware of the tremendous increase of people who are searching for another way to live. Ask people you know if they feel that time is speeding up and overwhelmingly the answer is "yes." What they are receiving is a signal from the second component of the mind—the subconscious—that something is "changing."

The subconscious mind provides many "maintenance" functions for the physical body. Especially important is that the subconscious records and plays back our tapes of negative and positive programming. This programming can hold us in stagnation or stimulate us to grow. There is a distinct relationship between our subconscious mind and the influences of the astral body. This connection to our emotions can help or hinder our spiritual growth in ways that are hidden to us. Again, this relationship is directly affected by the Angelic Attunement.

Look around you, and take an inventory of your family and friends who have recently increased their learning about spiritual matters. This awareness is opening many to a passionate quest to contact the third aspect of mind— the superconscious.

The superconscious has many names in many cultures: the Christ within, the I AM consciousness, the Higher Self. I also like to call it the angelic presence within us. To be in contact with the superconscious means to be communing with the all-knowing mind of God. This connection resides in the superconscious mind and, therefore, exists in each one of us. We, thus, have the potential to tap into the wisdom of God within us.

By contacting the superconscious one can actually change the programming of the subconscious mind, thereby making one able to change the emotional and thinking patterns focused in the astral body and the health of the physical. This is the essence of the transformation that occurs during an Angelic Attunement. It is an energy technique that assists in transforming and aligning these seven elements of the human being for accelerated spiritual growth and awareness.

The seventh and last component of our sevenfold nature is the soul. The soul is a glorious vibration that is of the world of spirit; in fact, at the time of death, the soul doesn't "leave" to go to the spirit world. It is already in the spirit world. This is the component of our make-up which is divine and eternal.

In the beginning when each of us was created, we emerged from the source as extensions of the Creator. The soul is the part of us that remains connected to God. We were each given a separate soul so that we could experience God individually. The purpose of our creation was so that we could know the love and wisdom of God. Once the experience was completed, we were to return back to the source.

But we strayed from the original plan and, as a result, the soul is basically waiting for the other six components to "get their act together," so the personality can become perfected. Once that perfection is achieved, the soul can ascend and again become part of the source from which it first originated. One can envision the soul as the candlelight that is kept in the window so that we are able to find our way home.

An Angelic Attunement is a technique that assists us in working toward our own perfection by blending these seven components harmoniously, so that they function as a whole, rather than independently. When you experience a successful Angelic Attunement, the resulting inner harmony is also felt within the life force of Mother Earth and is of great comfort to her in this time of exploitation. It is my belief that peace on earth must begin with peace in each of us. An Angelic Attunement helps to maintain an experience of profound peace in body, mind, and spirit.

The energies of the mind are aligned so that your thoughts can be more creative and you can connect more directly with the mind of God. The Angelic Attunement can help to replace illusionary thoughts of imperfection with the truth of your divinity as a child of God. The physical body is aligned so that you reflect radiant health and the youthful appearance of the God presence within you.

The alignment also works toward transmuting and transforming all kinds of malfunctions of the physical body on atomic and cellular levels. The emotions are aligned as the Angelic Attunement raises you into the harmonious emotions of higher octaves of perfection; for example, the peace, love, happiness, and joy of the angels. The alignment of the soul establishes a new etheric blueprint that will reflect the divine plan for your life and help you achieve oneness with God.

In their book *Meditation and the Mind of Man*, Herbert B. Puryear and Mark A. Thurston sum up this thought by saying, "Our work in the earth, then, is to become one, thus one with God by integrating the activities of the body, mind, and soul. When this harmony is attained, there is an attunement that allows God to manifest in His fullness through us."[4]

The manner in which the angels transform and energize you during the Attunement is by use of "radiation" energy, which works like a magnet to harmonize your body, mind, and soul and to attract to you the honorable goal that you determined for yourself prior to your Attunement.

Let me expand upon the concept of this radiation of God's energy so that you fully understand the power behind an Attunement. Angels serve God by radiating the specific ideal they embody. This radiation embodies a quality or positive energy which resonates in tune with the Creator. The angels learn through controlling their radiation how to "become" their ministration or their service to an ideal.

An interesting way to appreciate how angels "radiate" these ideals to us is by understanding how they teach other angels. It's not commonly known, but angels who desire to work in service to the earth are actually taught by other angels whose service and responsibility it is to see to the outworking of God's plan. They teach the angels how to draw the radiation from the heart of the Divine Creator and how to emulate and radiate a "feeling" of the ideal.

The teacher angel who is in charge of the student angels radiates the "feeling" to the students. Let us use the example of "truth." The color, nature, and energy of truth passes telepathically from the teacher to the students who absorb the quality into their own inner essence. The students then *become* that quality—holding the ideal—as they feel this radiation soaring through their beings. They continue to learn, under the tutelage of their teacher, how to hold this quality within their angelic bodies for longer and longer periods of time.

Once it is determined that they are able to hold the radiation, they are then assigned to a more experienced member of the angelic kingdom who is working in service to the people on earth. The novice angel is asked to hold the quality within until the directing angel chooses an individual who is to be the recipient of the radiation. Once it is determined that the novice angel is able to follow through on sending forth a particular radiation, that angel is assigned to the earth in service to that particular ideal or radiation.

As the novice angels continue to grow in their abilities, they become vested with enough control of their energy to be given, for example, the care of a home, a church, or a hospital. With this assignment they act just as they did for an individual, except that they remain as a constant broadcaster of their radiation at the particular location of their assignment. They draw upon the energy of God to bless whomever or whatever they are in charge of, and send forth their radiation to all the inhabitants of that location.

Through their facility with radiation, the angels are concerned with bringing the gifts of God to earth, and they are very determined in their focus. Because of this desire to assist in the transformation of those humans who are seeking the realization of their own divinity, the angels have offered us the radiation of Angelic Attunements.

St. Francis of Assisi had an experience that I feel reflects the way radiation works. He had invited a young brother in the monastery to join him when he preached to the people in the village. The two of them walked through the village, all the while conversing with each other on numerous spiritual topics. Upon turning homeward to the monastery, the young brother realized that because they both had been so absorbed in their conversation, they had not preached in the village. St. Francis responded that as they walked, the people had watched them and overheard bits and pieces of their conversation, and had noticed clearly that they were talking about the love of God. So it didn't really matter what St. Francis was doing because he was one with God. This oneness radiated from him in the same manner that it had been radiated to him.[5] He was "attuned" to God.

I have heard people remark, "Hold that thought," and I think that's an appropriate way to describe what the angels do. God may tell an angel, for example, to hold the thought of "faith" and the angel does it exactly. It becomes the pure essence of faith and is able to emulate that essence to all who are in need of faith.

So when you think that you need the angels' assistance to supply you with faith in order to handle a particular problem in your life, the angels that emulate faith will connect with you and shower you with the radiation of faith. Whatever quality they are told to manifest, they become that quality with their entire consciousness and radiate it endlessly. This is how the angels are able to do such penetrating work during Angelic Attunements.

Even though Angelic Attunements are often conducted by someone such as myself, I have adapted the methods I use so that you can work with the Attunement energy on your own. Following the instructions, I'll give you some pointers that can help you succeed.

Recognizing ourselves as children of God and brothers and sisters of the Christ is a key facet of Angelic Attunements. It is moving toward the realization that we are joint heirs with Christ to all that God has and is.

Edgar Cayce described this concept as an *equality* with God: "Every experience is an assurance. And as He has given, Behold the face of the angels ever stands before the throne of God; the awareness in self that thou may be one with, equal with, the Father-God, as His child, as the brother of the Christ . . . And as the awareness comes, it is as the angel of hope . . . " (2533-7)

The reading beautifully illustrates how the angels, who are always near the throne of God, radiate an assurance and an awareness of our oneness with God.

Charles Fillmore describes the Christ as the "incarnating principle of the God-man; the perfect Word or idea of God, which unfolds into the true man and is blessed with eternal life."[6]

An Angelic Attunement moves an individual closer to the self-realization that we are all perfect ideas of God. Keep this in mind as you proceed. (Though you may have someone read the procedure to you, I suggest you try to experience the Attunement energy as you read. You may also study the experience in the pages to come, then follow it from memory in your meditation.)

Angelic Attunement Meditation

Find a space in your home where you will not be disturbed. Consecrate the area by lighting a candle in honor of the source of all life. Allow yourself to relax in the moment. Know that in the divine order of all creation there is radiating an energy of oneness. All life expresses the fullness of the Creator. In this expression of oneness the angelic host offer themselves in service to God to allow heaven to come to earth through Angelic Attunements.

Express in a personal prayer your desire to participate in this Angelic Attunement. State your decree.

As you continue to relax, turn your heart and your mind to the angels—messengers from the Source of all light. In a beautiful communion with the angels, feel the light within you grow ever brighter and more radiant until it illumines every inch of your being. Know that as you do this, divine light is radiating from within you, above you, below you, around you. Visualize this now.

Imagine that you are now one with the light. Let the light of the angels shine through you. Know that by attuning

with them you are attuning to a greater spiritual awareness. Visualize this awareness and feel it, as it grows like a
seed within you. Feel the radiation of the angels as it is
planted in your consciousness and is nourished by the faith
and love of the angels. The radiation spreads, expands, and
grows within you.

The experience has been described by David Spangler in
his book *Attunement*: "I realize that this Awareness of
limitless Love is not outside of me; it has a lower octave
counterpart within me. I must find that counterpart and
place; it's like striking middle C in order to hear through
resonance a higher C note."[7] The angels are striking the key
of love within you so that you may experience the angelic
realm through resonating to the vibration of the angels'
love for you.

Now use your imagination and feel your consciousness
rising higher and higher into realms of light. You are
ascending into the higher octaves of the angelic realm.
Picture a golden white light spinning around your feet and
ankles. This beautiful spiraling vortex of energy builds and
builds, rising up through your legs and enveloping your
body. Believe it to be possible, and it will be—for the angels
are there with you.

Your entire body is being surrounded by this glorious
white light. Feel yourself at peace—at one—attuned to the
realm of angelic light. Slowly let the light from your feet
spiral back down to the ground; however, remain attuned
to the eternal angelic light. Allow yourself to be in the midst
of a spiraling vortex of energy from below your feet to
above your head, as you open yourself to the unity of all
kingdoms. Allow yourself to lose all sense of whether you
are a man or a woman, as you become more and more
aware that you are light.

Your seven bodies are now being aligned by the angels—they are forming a channel of one focused conscious effort through which God's highest good for you will flow. Nothing can encumber this goodness—no human thought, feelings, or words. Allow the radiation of the angels to grow and grow as you become more sensitive to their subtle vibration.

Remember that the Attunement releases old patterns of separation. You are becoming aligned with the truth of God's greatness in your life. Allow all your fears, anger, frustrations, and resentments to be transmuted by the angels into pure light.

As the Attunement is taking place, allow yourself to sense that you are not alone. Realize you have never been alone and will never feel alone again. The love of the angels surrounds you and protects you always. A host of thousands of angels are about you. The Attunement makes you aware that all of God's gifts are available to you at all times. It is only our human limited perception that keeps us from realizing this and expressing God's highest good in all areas of our life.

Feel yourself attuned with the one breath of God, the one heartbeat of God. You are absorbing the God qualities into your being through this Attunement, which is cleaning your seven vehicles and helping you build for yourself a true God-Reality. Know that the angels bring you the experience of the wholeness of God—perfect health, harmony, peace, love, and joy. There is but one presence and that is the spirit of God's love.

That love is now anchoring into your seven lower vehicles and will radiate the message of God's love to all those with whom you come in contact. The radiation will become the power of attraction, drawing to you all the honorable ideals that you want for yourself.

Know that through this Attunement the path you walk

will lead you only to the actualization of your highest good. The thoughts you have will insure the expression of your highest good. The angels decree that you shall experience God's highest good for you in all that you see, feel, and speak.

Feel yourself blending with the kingdom of the angels. Know that directed to you is a one-pointed consciousness, which is the angels serving God by radiating to you the message that you are loved.

Feel the angelic energy building around you. Feel that energy accelerate. Know that as the energy continues to build the fulfillment of God's will in your life is made clearer and clearer. Let the gift of clarity manifest. The higher frequency of light from the angels will enable you to know beyond any doubt that the angels' energy is flowing in, through, and around you. Allow a greater understanding of the truth for your own life; rejoice in your spiritual growth and your inner beauty. Feel the blessing of divine order being given to your life. Feel the fullness of God.

Your life is being charged with the beautiful golden light of the angels. Every avenue of blessing is being opened to you that will assist you in realizing the reality of God within you. Intensified angelic radiation is attuning your seven lower vehicles, and the light of the angels is expanding. Your unlimited potential expands with it.

Remember that the entire angelic host stands at readiness to assist you. You will no longer accept limitation in your life. You know and accept this truth. From this moment forward you can experience a newness in your life, for you are God's masterpiece of life-expression.

The angels joyously radiate to you the energies of perfect life, peace, love, and joy. You are being transformed by their blessing of an Angelic Attunement. The angels are creating an attraction energy which is pouring throughout all the levels of your existence.

The angels' love and light illuminate your life and the lives of those around you. Where there may have been darkness, there is now only light. Know that the shining ones are radiating love to you. Feel yourself aglow with love, faith, and all that you need in your life. Feel yourself attuned to the vibration of that which you desire. Through this radiation you have been blessed and will bless others. Embracing this experience of an Angelic Attunement, gently return your focus to the eternal now.

Believe that a new-found joy, spiritual freedom, and fulfillment can be yours through the help of the angels. Step forth and welcome this new day enthusiastically. All is in divine order in your life. All is well with your soul. The glorious company of heaven is pouring forth their radiation to assist you in the fullest expression of your perfection.

Your seven bodies are unified together, forming a one-pointed consciousness through which the blessings of God may flow unencumbered into your thoughts, words, feelings, and actions. You are unlimited prosperity, success, health, love, intelligence, happiness, and joy. Feel the divine currents flowing in and through you. Feel the spiraling energy around you giving you an image of ascending and descending angels. Bringing the angelic energy back with you, become aware that within the feelings and energy you are sensing is the fulfillment of every good and perfect thing you desire.

Every cell, electron, atom, and every thought and feeling have been touched. A resurrection energy has been called forth within your very being. Your true divine identity has been resurrected by the energies of the Angelic Attunement. God's presence is now fully anchored in your seven bodies, and the transforming activity of His light is increasing every minute as you emerge from the Attunement experience. From this point forward, be open to receiving the divine directives, inspirations, and ideas that will assist you in the fulfillment of your divine plan.

✧ ✧ ✧

Through the regular use of Attunement energy you can increase your sense of oneness in all areas of your life until one day you discover that your life is in continual oneness with the universe. In other words, it is a means of helping seekers everywhere attain God Consciousness—oneness with the superconscious.

Once you begin working regularly with the Angelic Attunement energy, a realization occurs that your consciousness extends beyond this world. You'll discover that the boundary between you and God has vanished. You will finally experience what it's like to feel your own infinity, your own eternal place in the universe.

I have seen people who, as a result of the special experience of Angelic Attunements, attain improved financial freedom; create wonderful, loving relationships; restore their bodies to vibrant health; develop their highest spiritual potential; reach levels of excellence and success; attract the perfect buyer for their home; manifest promotions or changes in job positions. The list is endless, as is the power of the angels to help us on earth.

One particular Attunement experience I'd like to share involves a woman named Joanne. Joanne had been given the suggestion from a private session with a lightworker that there may be anger buried deep inside her that needed to be released in order to allow for her spiritual growth to continue. The lightworker recommended that she work with the angels to accomplish this, so she called me for an appointment.

Joanne warned me over the phone that it might be an "ugly" session due to what needed to be released, since her hidden anger was not easy to "get to." I remember the angels assuring me even as I spoke to her that there was nothing ugly in the eyes of God, only that which is void of light. Besides, I already knew that it is never difficult to get to the truth—not while the angels are around.

As Joanne and I began the Attunement, I could see that she was immediately surrounded by her own Guardian Angel and the angels of service who came forth to assist in the session. There was standing room only! I immediately thought that the angelic crowd was being provided to assist Joanne.

However, Joanne and I both were soon shown that there was no anger that needed to be released; rather it was Joanne's need to take hold of and claim for herself the innate perfection of her immortal soul. Joanne's blessed little voice spoke through tears of love, "God is telling me I am perfect." She was crying; I was crying, too, as once again it was shown to us that "Father knows best."

The love that is radiated through Attunements goes beyond words. It just "is." Through this Attunement, whatever hidden anger the lightworker saw in Joanne was healed—it had vanished and Joanne's life was changed.

These, of course, are the ideal Attunement experiences. It's important for you to know that a successful Attunement may not happen every time—either with a conductor or working alone. Success with an Angelic Attunement is not guaranteed, because while the angels are ever ready to work with you, there are some requirements that need to be fulfilled.

I have found that when people are in a state of denial about their need to work on themselves, the angels will wisely help them fall asleep during the Attunement! Some people ask for Attunements and expect the angels to do all the work. They want the angels to "wave a magic wand" and make it happen without the individual participating. If people don't really believe at the heart level that an Angelic Attunement is possible, the angels will pull a veil down over their consciousness and again they will go to sleep.

If you are not ready consciously to attune to the energy, the angels will respect your highest good and not override your free will. When this happens, I still believe that you receive Attunement energy, but on an unconscious level. The angels never withhold energy or their love from you; they simply deliver it in the vibrational frequency appropriate for your highest good. The individual may not feel anything consciously, but the angels never fail to shower their love upon anyone who asks.

Ultimately, in order for the Attunement to work, you will need to dedicate yourself to the oneness of life by taking time to pray and meditate regularly. You also need to make time, and take the steps, to repeat your work with the Attunement energy, as the demands of the outer world and your lower personality begin to creep into your consciousness once again with their negativity.

The more you experiment with Angelic Attunements, the more you will be able to communicate telepathically with the angelic realms. Angelic Attunements are much more than communication opportunities and more than healing sessions. They are experiences of communion.

As you work with the Attunement energy, you can climb higher and higher into your own consciousness, and—if you have faith—the angels will help you every step of the way. As you progress toward making genuine positive changes in your life, know that with every ending is a new beginning—this is the gift that an Angelic Attunement can bring.

Once you've experienced a successful Angelic Attunement, let the angels guide you to achieve your goals in every area of your life. The seven components of your body, mind, and spirit are filled with vibrant energy. The full momentum of God's light is with you and will assist you in moving out of the old and into the new you. You are now able to release old patterns and conditions of fear. Your old sense of frustration can drop away forever.

As you seek an Angelic Attunement in your life, allow yourself to experience all the glory, all the perfection, and all the beauty which is your divine heritage. Know that God Himself can pulsate healing and abundance within you. Through the Attunement the angels will offer themselves in service as the sacred hand of God to re-establish in your life the divine plan fulfilled.

Let the sacred hand touch you.

·CRIS ARBO·

Chapter Nine

Expect Angelic Blessings

*" . . . the Lord thy God turned the curse into a blessing
unto thee, because the Lord thy God loved thee."*
Deuteronomy 23:5

The angels are reflections of the light and abundance of
God, and they love nothing better than to go into God's
"kitchen" and "cook up" something good for us. They are
always cooking up goodness, either by making miracles or
baking blessings. The problem is that not enough people
realize it. The angels circle round each of us, whether we're
aware of it or not, blessing us with guidance, protection,
and love. After all, as children of God, we are entitled by
heritage to receive the dearest, best desires of our hearts.

Fr. Pascal P. Parente in his book, *Beyond Space*, clearly
described the work of the angels in the following words:
"The holy Angels whom a merciful Father has assigned to
each of us shall escort us on this journey; they go before us
protecting and defending and leading us in this life . . . "[1]
I, too, have found this to be true. The angels protect us,
defend us, and guide us on our path—and that is truly a
blessing from God.

"Count Your Blessings" is a wonderful hymn that
poignantly reflects the importance of taking a regular
inventory of all the good in your life. The chorus of the song
goes like this: "Count your blessings—name them one by
one; count your many blessings and see what God has
done."[2]

A blessing is any gift from God that helps us in our lives.
Blessings can be people, places, sentiments, words, gifts,
favors, conditions, feelings, understandings, or miracles.
The best definition of a blessing is anything that brings a
measure of God's goodness to the recipient. It may be a
surprise that we weren't expecting or something for which
one hoped.

I have many blessings in my life, just as you do. God
loves me, and that's the most promising blessing of all. In
addition, God has given me the blessings of loving parents,
brothers and sisters, friends, a special someone, pets, a nice
home, a fulfilling job, clothes, and food.

Sometimes years pass before we realize that some of
what we've taken for granted have been blessings. Even
though I am not a parent myself, I have grown to appreciate
all that my mother and father did for me while I was
growing up. Of course, now I have to do those things for
myself, but even so, my parents were and still are a perpetual blessing in my life.

I receive an abundance of automotive blessings. My cars

oftentimes function on a "wing and a prayer." It seems that I am rarely excused from experiencing car problems, but I have occasionally been blessed by the location where they occurred. I have had my car very conveniently break down *at* the gas station while I was filling it. I have had a part fall off my car just as I drove up my driveway. On both occasions I was blessed by not being stranded with a disabled vehicle.

When the property issues of my divorce were settled, I obtained a mortgage for refinancing purposes. I had no idea, while I was going through the transition, that my divorce coincided with the lowest interest rates in ten years. This was an unexpected blessing in the midst of a very painful time in my life. The attorney at the settlement commented to me that I must have had a crystal ball to have known when to apply for that mortgage. Pointing toward heaven I smiled gratefully saying, "No, but He has one."

When you start counting blessings, you will be amazed how much you have to be thankful for, even if your life has been particularly hard. Focus on the blessings, for a change, and you will be able to accept the hardships as part of your life. I have seen people so engrossed in themselves and the negative aspects of life that they aren't able to spot a blessing when they see one. I encourage you to begin each day by counting your blessings and looking forward to all the new blessings that the angels can bring you to add to your list.

I want to share a little game I play with the angels. Whenever I spot a penny on the ground, I immediately thank the angels for a "heaven-sent-cent." To me, the penny is an outward sign from the angels that a blessing is imminent and I should be on the lookout. I'm always looking for those lost coins that become messages of "something's coming" for me. I think of them as pennies from heaven, and so are the blessings which follow.

There are blessings and miracles coming every second from the angels. The one that is the most exciting, however, is the miracle that is happening right inside of you as you read this book. As you read, you are opening your mind and your heart to the angelic kingdom, whose members are waiting to shower you with God's goodness and blessings.

How do we open ourselves to expect and receive angelic blessings? It is my belief that the very energy we impress upon our life and the lives of others emotionally and through our mental images and thoughts not only radiates forth from us into the world but returns back to us like a boomerang. As the Bible says: "Cast thy bread upon the waters: for thou shalt find it after many days." (Ecc. 11:1)

If you bless something, it will in turn bless you. If you damn or curse something, it will in turn curse you and be damning to you. How often have you heard someone, even yourself, say, "I hate my body"? Even if you find reason to be critical, you should bless your body instead. Even when you are not well, you should bless your body because of the positive energy you will send it.

I don't mean that you should bless the disease, as it is only a transitory expression, but to bless your life and all that is a part of your life: your home, your family, your office, your job. Do this, and the energy you sow in the "right now" you shall soon be reaping in the "right now" as well. The more blessings you acknowledge, the freer the angels will be to bestow more blessings upon you.

Blessings come in many forms. For example, the angels send blessings in the guise of compliments from others. Compliments are verbal blessings. Many people really need to learn how to accept these verbal blessings. When someone says to me, "You really look nice today, Janie," I return the compliment by saying, "Bless you." To me this action keeps the blessing energy flowing and acknowledges to the giver how much their words meant to me.

Learn to accept blessings graciously and to send blessings freely from yourself. Just as in days gone by when bucket brigades were formed to put out fires, we need to see ourselves as blessing brigades and keep the blessings flowing. Our blessing brigade will squelch the illusion that we are separated from each other and from God—from whom all blessings flow.

A dear friend of mine was having difficulty accepting blessings in his life. Whenever I would give this person a gift, he would immediately start telling me that I shouldn't have done it or he would apologize that he didn't have a gift for me. The angels encouraged me to help this man see the importance of being a gracious receiver as well as a gracious giver.

On one occasion when I had given him a present, he again started telling me that I shouldn't have gotten him anything. I took the gift I'd given him and said, "It's time you open yourself to receiving all that God wants to give you, and that means this gift from me!" I then handed the gift back to him. When I did, I could see a transformation taking place, as he finally let go and let God bless him with love in the form of my gift. This man has been so transformed in his attitude toward gifts that he recently asked me for a particular housewarming gift for his newly built home: a weathervane of Archangel Gabriel blowing his horn.

I love to bless people by remembering them with special gifts, and the angels have been especially resourceful in guiding me to find the perfect gift. I keep such a busy schedule that there is seldom enough time for shopping, but it is still important to me to show others the love I feel with presents for those who are blessings in my life.

I never hesitate to ask the "shopping angels" to help me find the perfect gift for someone I love. Once I put out the request, it never fails that within a few days an inspirational thought will be sent my way as to what the person would like. It's better than any shopping service available on earth. I get so excited when I receive the answer. Further, the time the angels have saved me is phenomenal. To me the angel shoppers save me legwork, thanks to *their* wing work.

It is important to see how sharing in someone else's joy is also a way of blessing that person. We all need to make certain we don't become bubble-busters when angelic blessings are received by others. There's an abundance of blessings available for all, so it's important not to be resentful when someone else receives good. God will never run out of miracles or blessings for us all.

Rev. Diane Berke, dean of The New Seminary in New York City, wisely states that the major obstacles to realizing blessings in our lives are fault-finding, complaining, and taking things for granted. Berke indicates that we can choose either to be fault-finders or love-finders. If we choose to be fault-finders, we tend to experience deprivation in our lives. But if we choose to be love-finders, we will experience blessings. So let's make up our minds to be love-finders every day.

In addition, be on the lookout for blessings in disguise. The angels love nothing better than to camouflage a blessing in what appears to be a setback or aggravation. On a recent trip to Philadelphia I was experiencing numerous problems in my train connections because one of the lines had been closed the day before. I ended up having to hire a cab to take me to my destination. As I was sitting in the cab feeling exhausted and frustrated, I wondered where the blessing could possibly be in all of this.

When I got to the conference, I met a fellow lecturer and was sharing my traveling tale of woe when he offered to drop me off in Baltimore on his way back to Virginia. As it turned out, the gentleman is the president of an association of metaphysical churches in the United States. He is also an absolute blessing in his own right. We had a most beneficial drive home, chatting together. As a result, I received an invitation from him to speak about the angels at an upcoming conference in Michigan. Now, I find it intriguing to know that any hardships I experience can soon become blessings in disguise.

Angels often provide blessings in the form of protection. How can the angels protect? When you're feeling the most vulnerable, they can use their powerful energy to surround you with a profound feeling of warmth that radiates with the message, "You are loved and you are not alone." They also can radiate a sense of fortification which says, "You are blessed with angelic protection. No harm can come to you." All you need to do is believe it, and be open to feeling it.

I know people who have been protected in mighty etheric fortresses of light provided by the angels. In one such case, a woman was being robbed at gunpoint. Even though she was conscious of her anxiety and fear, she was also aware of the uncanny energy of an angelic presence that was protecting her, assuring her that she would come to no harm. Even though her purse was stolen, no harm came to her physically. You can invoke the protection of the angels in any emergency situation.

Whenever you are having anxious moments in your life, turn your thoughts to the angels and ask for a blessing of protection. Let the angels assist you. They are always there to offer a shoulder or to help you carry your burden. Ask for angel relief from the problems you are facing. I call it "Angel-Ade." Just as it's helpful to know that when life gives me lemons, I can make lemonade, it's been equally helpful for me to know that I can mitigate my problems daily with "Angel-Ade."

Visualize putting your worldly concerns in the loving hands of the angels. When I feel myself overwhelmed by a problem, I will often say to the angels, "Please carry this for me for a while." Isn't that a wonderful blessing from God to have created a kingdom of glorious beings to help us through life?

One year I was on vacation at a dude ranch in Colorado. As part of the package, I was given the dubious privilege of being able to ride a horse named Dusty as much as I wanted during my week's stay. Dusty was an appropriate name for this horse, as I think he secretly conspired to "dust" me off at every opportunity. He did it under the conspiracy of wanting to eat every plant along the trail. Dusty loved to leisurely plod along the trail and then suddenly make a bee-line for a tasty-looking flower, where he would munch, munch, munch until he was finished. Once he found his chosen flower, he would come to a dead stop, showing no concern as to whether I stayed on top of him or joined the plant on the ground. Dusty would not even consider moving on until he was thoroughly finished eating every morsel of the plant.

On one particular day we were exploring a trail that took us up a small mountain range. Even though I was desperately trying to assert myself with Dusty, using every horse term I had ever heard Roy Rogers and Dale Evans utter, Dusty was still up to his antics of darting to every tasty-looking dandelion he saw.

During one particular meal madness, Dusty dashed with wild abandonment—or should I say, "Janie abandonment." I was hanging on for dear life when he came to a sudden stop at the edge of a cliff. I could feel myself lifting out of the saddle and heading for the edge, when suddenly the touch of an unseen hand took hold of my belt and yanked me back to safety. As Dusty bent his head to devour this latest delight that was blooming out over the cliff, I was breathlessly thanking the angels for saving me from the big roundup in the sky.

An equally protecting blessing came from my Guardian Angel during a winter ice storm. I was driving down a hill approaching a stop sign, when I gently put my foot on the brakes to stop at the end of the road. Because of an unseen patch of ice, when I lightly touched the brakes, the car went into a 360-degree spin right in the middle of the busy intersection. Where the car was going to end up, I wasn't certain. In the panic of the moment I wanted to slam on the brakes, but suddenly I heard the calm words of my wonderful Guardian Angel, who said, "*Don't* touch the brakes." I didn't question his guidance and felt a loving "grip" on my leg just to make certain that I had heard the words clearly. I let the car finish its spinning. It ended up going in the opposite direction, coming to a stop miraculously without hitting any other vehicles. Not only was there an angel driving my car that day, but several other cars as well.

The angels have also been wonderful in blessing me with guidance when I get lost while driving. One evening I was to be the guest speaker at a metaphysical church about an hour's drive from my home. I felt adequately prepared for the drive as I had gotten exact directions from one of the group's leaders.

As I was driving, however, it became obvious that something had been lost in the translation. I looked at my watch and saw that the time of my lecture was rapidly approaching. In a panic, I said to the angels, "I'm really lost! If you want me to talk to this group tonight about your kingdom, you'd better send help fast!" I had no sooner gotten the words out of my mouth when two women appeared walking together along the street. I rolled down my window and asked for directions. They knew exactly where I wanted to go and, furthermore, the quickest route to get there.

Angels not only bless us with support and wisdom, but they lift us from our doldrums with blessings of heavenly music, art, and other forms of inspiration. Saint Francis of Assisi was blessed when an angel appeared next to him holding a violin and bow in its hand. The angel told St. Francis that it would play for him as the angels play before the throne of God. The angel drew the bow across the violin string producing only a single note. St. Francis expressed that he was filled with such joy by that one sound that had there been any more his soul would have left his body.

I experienced a similar feeling of happiness when I first saw the photograph taken by John Wimberley entitled "Descending Angel." This photograph depicts one single foot gliding downward; it appears to belong to a beautiful heavenly angel about to set foot on the earth. When I first saw the photograph, I felt as if I was looking at a Renaissance work of art instead of a modern-day photograph.

"Descending Angel" took on even more meaning for me during a workshop experience in Guadalajara, Mexico. I was participating in a week-long workshop given by Dr. Fritz Smith, creator of a healing modality known as Zero Balancing. During that week Dr. Smith had arranged for a yoga instructor to lead us in morning exercises.

One afternoon Dr. Smith commented that this individual was not only a talented yoga instructor, but that he was a photographer as well. Dr. Smith then proceeded to hold up in front of the class a catalog of the young man's work. There on the front cover was "Descending Angel." I turned to the man in amazement and said, "You're the photographer of 'Descending Angel' "? I just knew that the blessed angels had arranged for our paths to cross on that remote mountaintop in Mexico.

In later conversations with him, I learned about his experience in photographing "Descending Angel" and how he felt that God had been the one holding the camera. To this day I thank the angels for giving me the opportunity to meet the artist who so honored the angels in his work.

Many artists and musicians have been blessed with visions of heaven, which they then shared with the rest of the world through their masterpieces. The composer George Friedrich Handel is said to have had such a vision when he composed his famous oratorio *The Messiah*. For twenty-four days he worked in seclusion. When the Hallelujah Chorus was completed, Handel is said to have exclaimed that he had seen heaven. How blessed the world has been for the gift of Handel's *Messiah!*

Fra Angelico, a great Renaissance artist known for his paintings of angels, was blessed with the experience of seeing angels in his room when he awoke from sleep. William Blake saw angels, and often included them in his poems and drawings. The world has been blessed ever since with Blake's drawings of angels, many of which, it has been said, give the impression that the angels actually posed for him. It's quite possible that they did!

The angels can also lead us to blessings that come in the form of "surprise" financial abundance. One woman came to me to ask the angels for advice in solving a financial problem. She was out of work, her bills were piling up, and money had just about run out. Her focus, as we began the session, was on what her life lacked.

After we prayed and meditated together, a message came through loud and clear. She was encouraged to give thanks for all God's blessings in her life and focus on what she had instead of on what she lacked. Through affirmations that the angels suggested, they guided her to open herself and be receptive to God's good which would be coming her way. She shrugged and went home.

Within a few weeks, she was surprised by an unexpected blessing in the form of a check. It was from her mortgage company, reimbursing her for overpayments that had amounted to several thousand dollars. This money enabled her to begin her life anew and restored her faith that God will always provide. We wondered afterward if the mortgage company would have found the error on their own—or if the intercession of the angels had somehow played a part. My vote is with the angels.

I, too, have experienced a surprise financial blessing. I have been employed for the past twenty years by a man who owns his own advertising agency specializing in equine advertising. He has been a blessing in my life because of the inspiration of his creative genius and the encouragement he has given me to believe in myself and be the best I can be.

When my marriage ended, this man whom I call my "Boss Angel" asked me into his office and said, "Now, is there anything you need financially because of the separation?" My employer is a very successful businessman who is always concerned with the bottom line, but on that morning he was truly an angel to me. He was looking for the bottom line of what I needed in my life. He is a man who has mastered the blending of his spiritual ideals with the demands of the material world.

The angels will deliver blessings when you may be feeling your lowest and need nothing short of a miracle to get you moving and back into life again.

A widow who came to the angels for a healing session was grief-stricken over the loss of her lifelong companion. She appeared to be in a state of depression when she arrived. Strangely, the angels suggested to her that she begin to volunteer her services at a nearby hospital. She began volunteering and became a blessing through her service. Her work blessed her with new-found joy, happiness, and friends.

No matter how impossible a situation appears to be or how desperate the circumstances, there is always a blessing to be found. This simple belief can make the difference between expecting the worst or expecting the best.

When Jacob was on his way to meet his brother, Esau, he wrestled with a "man" by a stream (Genesis 32:24-28). Many believe that this "man" was actually an angel, a messenger from God. After wrestling with him all night, Jacob won. At daybreak, when the man asked to be released, Jacob said, "I will not let thee go, except thou bless me." In response, the angel changed Jacob's name to Israel, which means "prince of God."

It is my belief that Jacob's fight with the angel symbolizes how we all fight with our fears. As Jacob feared Esau's revenge, we, too, wrestle with our doubts and fears until the dawn of truth and light enters our lives. As Jacob finally triumphed over his fears, so can we. The truth is, there is always a blessing in every struggle. We just need to look for it. Whatever challenge you are facing in your life, wrestle with it until it blesses you. Say to the angels, "I know there is good within this problem. Show me the blessing." As the angel did with Jacob, they will.

Never give up in your belief that a blessing is on its way. At one of my workshops a woman named Emma shared a most beautiful blessing that occurred in her life. What was special about this blessing was that it took twenty-five years for it to arrive. As a young woman, Emma had given birth to a daughter out of wedlock and then gave the child up for adoption. Years later, she met and married a wonderful man. Because of the genuine love between them, she openly shared the loss she felt in her life because of this daughter whom she had given up. She ached inside to know where she was and if she was all right. Her husband supported her in her quest to find her daughter, but the task seemed impossible.

For years Emma and her husband tried every possible way to track down this lost daughter. Because of the conditions of the adoption, Emma was not allowed access to the information she needed; namely, the names and address of the adoptive parents. But Emma never stopped searching and never stopped praying to God for a miracle in her life. She told her husband that before she died she would be reunited with her daughter.

One day, Emma was inspired to run a newspaper ad in the town where she had given birth to the child some twenty years before. In her ad she appealed to any young woman in that town who had been born on the date of her daughter's birth and who had been raised by adoptive parents. It was her hope that her daughter or someone who knew her would read the ad.

When Emma gave birth to the child, she had felt deep shame for having it out of wedlock. She hadn't wanted any of her family members to know about the birth, so on the birth certificate she gave only her name and no information about her family. Even if the daughter had wanted to find Emma and would have had the courts open her files, she could only have found Emma's name and a false birthplace.

The daughter did not see the ad. The reason, as Emma

would later learn, was that the daughter had moved a total of eight times across the country since she was adopted, and no longer lived in the town. But someone else did see the ad. It was a woman who works with a mysterious man known simply as the "Silent Watcher," who works anonymously to help people find lost children in various cities on the East Coast.

The woman called Emma and explained that the "Silent Watcher" could find her daughter, as he had sources available to him that were not available to the average citizen. The woman went on to say that little information is known about the "Silent Watcher" other than he has made it his life's work to find missing persons. There was a fee involved for his time, and Emma was advised of the cost. The woman asked if Emma would be interested in having the "Silent Watcher" call her. With doubts in her mind, Emma agreed.

Shortly thereafter, Emma received a phone call from the man who explained that Emma would never meet him and never be able to call him. He would call Emma. Emma gave him the little bit of information she had—the town where she gave birth and the date and time of the birth. It was agreed that when she received a phone call saying that the daughter had been located, she would have to wire the money to the name and address of the woman who had made the initial contact. Once the money had been received, Emma would be put in touch with the daughter. The "Silent Watcher" said he would call her again when her daughter was found.

The "Silent Watcher" imposed one additional condition which Emma had to clearly understand and accept without compromise. If it was discovered that the daughter was addicted to drugs, no information would be given to the mother. It would then be expected that Emma would stop pursuing information from the "Silent Watcher." Emma prayed that this wouldn't be so.

Within twenty-one days, Emma received a phone call. She was told that her daughter was alive and well, that she was married and had three children of her own. She was then told the name of the town her daughter lived in. The "Silent Watcher" also teased Emma because Emma had thought she had given birth late on October 10; instead, in her anxious and confused state, she had lost track of time and the birth actually occurred minutes into the early morning of October 11. The "Silent Watcher" informed Emma of all the places her daughter had lived in throughout the country because of the move of her adoptive parents and husband. Emma was advised to take her leap of faith and wire the money. Once the money was received, the "Silent Watcher" would put Emma in touch with her daughter.

Emma wired the money on a Friday morning and by the time Monday evening came, she had not received a call from her daughter or anyone. Emma was beginning to think she had been tricked. She told her husband that even if that was the case, she would do it all over again in the hope of finding her daughter.

Emma called the woman on Monday evening and expressed her concern about not hearing anything after having wired the money. But the woman excitedly told Emma to hang up the phone as a call was on its way to her.

Within minutes the "Silent Watcher" called and gave Emma the name and number of her daughter, and asked Emma to call right away as the daughter was waiting by the phone. Apparently the daughter had been out of town over the weekend and it was only earlier on Monday evening that the "Silent Watcher" had been able to tell her about the phone call that would be forthcoming from her natural mother.

With her heart pounding in anticipation, Emma called her daughter immediately and the beautiful reuniting of mother and child began. They talked on the phone—long-distance—the entire night. They were finally reunited, physically, within a month's time, when Emma and her husband bought plane tickets to visit her daughter, son-in-law, and grandchildren.

Emma never gave up faith that she would find her daughter. She heeded the message to place her ad and never stopped expecting that the blessing would arrive. The angels of service heard her prayers, even though it took twenty-five years to fulfill. She recently shared with me what an extreme joy it was to celebrate a recent Thanksgiving with all her children and grandchildren—including her precious firstborn.

Just like Emma, I've never stopped looking for blessings in the form of miracles. A Cayce reading encourages us to follow the angels' example and let our lives overflow with "the real *joy* of living." (1159-1) One of the greatest joys in life is when we overflow with the knowledge that blessings and miracles are real for each and every one of us.

Start today to deliver blessing messages to others. I think three of the sweetest words that can be spoken are "God bless you." As you look outward at all of God's creation, bless it. Bless all the people and all the conditions in your life, whether they seem good or bad. Look for good in everyone and everything. Whatever you are doing in your life, bless it and thank God for it. As you rise from your bed in the morning, bless the day. As you put on your clothes, bless them.

There is nothing more beautiful to me than hearing stories about how the angels have spoken to people through others at just the right time. Just as God sends the angels, the angels often send human messengers who deliver cogent words of advice or comfort when someone needs them the most.

Someone did this for me when I was feeling anxious about a particular workshop I was hosting. There was going to be a person attending the workshop who made me very uncomfortable. Even though I was trying my best to send out unconditional love, I was still inwardly dreading the encounter.

Just before the workshop started, Ann, a dear friend of mine who hadn't planned on attending, appeared unexpectedly, announcing that she had a sudden desire to join us. Ann had been practicing her meditations with the angels for years and was now able to hear their messages regularly. Her words were as follows: "I really don't know why I'm here other than the angels said you needed me. They said to get over here as quickly as possible, so here I am." Privately, I shared my anxiety and told her how much her presence meant to me in getting through the evening.

Sometimes we get so caught up in our emotions that the help we would receive from on high just can't get through. Our own human tension blocks the way. It is at those times that the angels send the earthly cavalry in to break down our barriers. Ann had truly been such a blessing that night.

I also want to share another belief I have about opening ourselves to receiving blessing messages. Whenever we are hungry, we do not hesitate to feed ourselves. For some that means three meals a day or more. But how often do you feed your spiritual hunger? Are you blessing your mind with inspirational thoughts? I challenge you to take spiritual food, and nourish and bless your soul just as often as you take food for your body. I developed my angelic cards because I believe that we each need spiritual tools in our lives to help us fine-tune our ability to these messages and blessings.

The importance of positive and inspirational thoughts was re-enforced for me when I conducted an angel healing session with a client who was opening a massage practice. This woman was anxious over whether her business would be a success and whether she'd receive her wish to be of service. The angels encouraged her to calm her anxiety through the use of a daily affirmation, "God is blessing and healing the world through my massage practice." What she affirmed was soon accomplished, because not only did her business prosper, but her clients are unanimous that this woman is truly a blessing and healing force in their lives.

The angels have shared with me many different meditations that would bless our lives if we would only use them. One of the most renewing meditations you can participate in is called an "Angelic Blessing Bath and Shower of Love." Just as God heals the earth with showers of rain, "Angelic Blessing Baths" renew us when our spirits are low or our souls parched. When we desperately need the waters of God's love to flow through us, refresh us, and revive us back to life, an "Angelic Blessing Bath" is the answer.

Try to picture the images as you read the following meditation, and let the experience become real for you.

"Angelic Blessing Bath and Shower of Love" Meditation

Begin by visualizing shimmering divine angelic white light. Breathe this light into your heart and, when you exhale, feel the angelic light expanding throughout your body. Repeat this several times as the light expands to increasingly intense levels.

Speaking from your heart, make your intent known to the angelic kingdom: "I call for the presence of the Archangels, Angels, Devas, Elementals, and all the Angelic Host of Light who wish to assist me in the 'Angelic Blessing Bath and Shower of Love' meditation for the highest good of all."

Visualize a single drop of angelic water descending from above you. This drop of water falls upon your head and blesses you with purity. As it splashes on your head, more drops follow, and then it expands farther so that you are now seeing a stream of water drops washing down over you from the top of your head to the base of your spine, and continuing on to your feet and into the ground beneath you. As the stream washes over you, you are receiving the angels' blessing of purification. The angels are purifying all your thoughts, feelings, words, actions, and reactions, blessing them with the essence of God's goodness.

Now as the stream of angelic water turns into a river, visualize your body and mind being simultaneously raised in vibration. Feel yourself purified, balanced, and charged with God's desire of perfection for you. You are being aligned with the peace, love, and harmony of the angelic kingdom. As the river becomes a flood, feel this energy of perfection pouring inside you, splashing around you, gurgling beneath you and above you.

The flood of angelic water intensifies within you, and suddenly you become aware of the presence of a magnificent Archangel. It is beloved Gabriel, standing radiantly behind you. In the midst of the angelic bath, he showers you with love. He places his hands upon your shoulders and blesses you on the right side with God's love and on the left side with your own God-given power to love. Now, he places his hands upon the top of your head and blesses you with the wisdom of God. You feel the energy of God's love shower you, the power of God emerging within you. You feel the wisdom of God bathing you with illumination from the top of your head to the tips of your feet. Within your being there is an awakening of your spiritual energy as every cell, atom, and molecule is filled with the brilliant, vibrating energy of God's shower. You are being bathed in a new, heightened awareness of your true identity. You perceive yourself as God's name—I AM THAT I AM—in expression.

You become aware that Archangel Gabriel is now standing in front of you with outstretched arms handing you a glowing golden key. Gabriel speaks, "Oh, sweet being of light. How you serve is the key."

Gabriel places the golden key in your hands. As you gaze upon this key, you feel the shower turn into a shaft of pure white light, descending from heaven until it reaches the point of light in your heart where you started. This shaft of light penetrates the point of light in your heart and takes on the image of a seed. This is the seed of the "Immaculate Concept" of your divine plan within you. With the light of God above you connecting with the light of God within you, you are now lifted into an awareness of your purpose and service to yourself and others on the earth. Your body and consciousness are now accepting God's original plan of perfection for you. You are seeing the "Immaculate Concept" in your life with en"light"enment and clarity.

Gabriel announces that you are blessed among the children on earth, for within your being is a seed of service to which only you can give birth. Feel yourself blend with the message of Gabriel and the truth that you are a blessing to yourself and to all whose lives you touch. You are the radiant expression of God.

You look once again at the key, and Gabriel says that this key symbolizes your freedom to open any door that you want opened in your life. If you want perfect health, the door will open and you will be blessed with vibrant health.

If you want success and fulfillment in your career, the door will be opened and you will be blessed with achievement. If you want an improved relationship, the door will be opened and you will be blessed with a loving companion.

This key is a key of service to yourself and to the planet. You hold the key to any honorable goal that you want in your life. You choose the doors that you want to open and the doors that you want to keep locked. You hold the key to a life of abundant blessings in your hands. Hold this image of abundant blessings in your heart, too, and in your mind as you gently bring your focus back to the room . . . this life . . . this plane of service.

✤ ✤ ✤

It's important that all people everywhere—especially you—should not only believe in the possibility of blessings, but that you should *expect* them in your life. As a beloved son or daughter of God, it is your birthright to expect all the love that God has to offer, and it is the angels who would deliver that love more freely—if you would but open your awareness to their sincerity. It's not childish or foolish to expect the angels to bless you, help you, and surprise you. Above all, believe that you deserve it, and you will begin to notice blessings in your life.

Archangel Gabriel encourages me to make one last statement before this chapter comes to a close. He wants me to tell you to be on the lookout for a key in the days and weeks ahead. It will be a key that you can place on your altar to remind you that you are the "key" ingredient in God's divine plan for your life—and that you are also the key to helping the angels provide blessings to those around you, especially those who haven't yet opened their minds to the reality of the angels in their lives.

Chapter Ten

Be an Angel

*"Be not forgetful to entertain strangers: for thereby some
have entertained angels unawares."*
Hebrews 13:2

A little boy named John was fascinated by the sermon he
had just heard on the angels, because the famous quote
from Hebrews had given him definite ideas about how the
angels dress. He was telling a friend about it when the two
of them got into an argument. The little friend insisted that
all angels had for their heavenly attire were wings, but little
John disagreed.

"It isn't true," insisted John. "Our preacher says that
some of them are strangers in underwear."[1]

If angels are able to take on human form and camouflage
themselves as "strangers," what would be our giveaway
that these are truly angelic beings in human disguise?

What is a distinctive characteristic of angels that we can look for that would signal that we are entertaining "angels unawares"? You can sum it up in one word: SERVICE.

Angels are servants to God. They serve God in all that they do. If we want to express angelic energy in our own lives, then we need to become masters of service. Flower A. Newhouse beautifully expressed it when she wrote, "Our inward and outward striving receives new encouragement every time we pause to deeply consider Angelic magnitudes of selfless service performed in the 'beauty of holiness.'"[2]

One of my favorite quotations from the Bible is when Jesus said to His disciples, "But he that is greatest among you shall be your servant." (Matthew 23:11) Jesus was telling us that to serve is the most important thing we can do in our lives.

Alice A. Bailey, channeling the ascended master Djwhal Khul in the book *Ponder on This*, stated that "This Law of Service was expressed for the first time fully by the Christ, two thousand years ago ... Today, we have a world which is steadily coming to the realization that 'no man liveth unto himself,' and that only ... in service, can man begin to measure up to his innate capacity."[3]

Albert Einstein captured that same reflection of the importance of service when he wrote, "The high destiny of the individual is to serve rather than to rule ... "[4]

As I have shared in earlier chapters, the angels do not concern themselves with rank—who is the highest and lowest of their kingdom. Their intent is to perform the task for which they were created by God. Nothing distracts them from fulfilling their service to God.

When I read the Cayce reading 2300-1, the words become a battle cry for the servers of the angelic kingdom and the world as well. Cayce's energetic statement, "Let thy watchword be, *'Use me, O Lord—use me!'* " is a proclamation to God asking that our lives be ones of service to the divine plan. In reading 1710-10, Cayce offers the following affirmation to aid us in developing our lives through service as a blessing to others: "O Lord, let me in body, mind and in purpose keep Thy ways, in such a manner as to be a channel of blessings ever to others—in His name."

Colonel James B. Irwin, a former astronaut who was part of a crew who walked on the moon, often explains when speaking at conferences the revelation he had en route back to planet earth. He realized that his life's "mission" was to be a servant—not a celebrity—and that his purpose is to share his experiences with others so they may come to know God's glory.

We receive the opportunity daily to choose between the call of our Higher Self to serve God and the call of the ego to serve the "little self." To the "little self" or ego personality, work and service are sometimes seen as a curse. To the Higher Self, service is an opportunity to give not only to God but to yourself as well. Henry David Thoreau once said that when people choose their labor, they are choosing their future self. Any service, even in the form of labor, if given freely, gives you the chance to reveal to the world the magnificent, perfect you that God already knows you to be.

The angels know that whatever their assignment may be, they are serving God. Likewise, whatever we are doing in our lives, whether we are fixing dinner, carpooling children, cleaning the house, mowing the lawn, or pulling weeds, we, too, should feel that we are doing our work in service and honor to everyone and, therefore, to God.

In answer to the question, "How do the angels help us?" Methodist church founder John Wesley stated, "In a thousand ways . . . they may assist us in our searching after truth, remove many doubts and difficulties . . . They may warn us of evil in disguise, and place what is good in a clear, strong light. They may gently move our will to embrace what is good, and to fly from that which is evil . . . "[5]

Just like the angels, there are a "thousand ways" in which we may assist and serve God in our lives. Angels are messengers who spread the word of God's love, but we can be angels, too, increasing our own blessings and those of others.

It seems sad that not enough people know that they should expect blessings and miracles from the angels, but it's even sadder to realize that because they don't believe, these miracles and blessings aren't shared with others either. The truth is that you are blessed to be a blessing and to serve. Edgar Cayce shared the importance of this message in reading 3161-1: "To be a channel of blessing to others is that purpose for which each soul has come into conscious activity in a material world."

I truly do believe that we are blessed to be blessings and so, in response to a message from the angels, the license plate on my car reads: "BLESSIN." As I drive this car, I like to think that all who read these plates connect with the thought of blessings in their life.

There was one particularly humorous meditation in which the angels pointed out to me that you can sum up all life experiences with these words: "Lessons and blessin's." We are here on earth to learn specific lessons and to open ourselves to receiving the benefits which God gives bountifully to us.

In what specific ways can someone "be an angel" and serve? What are some things you can do to be an angel of service on earth? Angels are constantly singing praises to God. So you can be an angel by saying thanks to God for all the blessings in your life. Tell people in your life that you are thankful to them and for all that they do for you. Angels radiate the truth and the divine principles of God. You can be an angel by being true to your own truth and ideals. Angels touch us with their warmth. You can be an angel by touching and hugging someone, and sharing your warmth. If you dare, try to find someone in your life today with whom you can share a hug. Lessons in service are apparent everywhere; all you have to do is open your heart to them.

One of the best lessons on the importance of service was taught by Jesus during the Last Supper. The lesson must have seemed strange to His disciples, when He took a towel and proceeded to wash their feet. "If I then, your Lord and Master, have washed your feet; ye also ought to wash one another's feet." (John 13:14)

I am a member of a women's healing and prayer group. At one of our meetings we gathered soothing herbs and oils, filled containers with water, and gave each other foot massages and foot baths. We did this healing service to remind ourselves to follow Jesus' example by serving others.

Angels know no pain, suffering, or sense of separation, so be an angel by letting go of old hurts and wounds, and accepting healing in your life. The angels uplift and inspire us to recognize our true divinity. You, too, can be an angel by inspiring someone with encouragement.

The angels are ministering spirits. They minister to our needs by bringing us messages of hope and joy. By writing a letter of joy or sending a card of hope to someone who needs it, you can be an angel, too. When you go to a card store to buy an occasion card for a family member, why not stop and think of someone you know who could use a lift? When I was going through my separation, many people inspired me with beautiful cards and thoughtful gestures. Some of the cards I received at that time I still rejoice over today.

I have always been notorious for not liking to cook. It is a source of constant teasing from my friends. When we have our women's meetings, we rotate the location, and the hostess for each meeting is responsible for providing food. As it happens, many of the ladies in our group are talented cooks and make wonderful refreshments. When it's my turn, however, my friends tease me, saying if Janie says she "made it" it means she "made it" from the bakery to the car.

During my separation, many friends and family members invited me to dine with them. I laugh as I think of the friends who would call and ask if "Janie the Foodless" would like to come to dinner. Perhaps there is someone you know who needs the fellowship of your family at dinner. Let me tell you, that's a *great* way to be of service to someone who doesn't like pots and pans.

Angels give us unexpected blessings, and you can be an angel by providing someone with a surprise when that person needs it the most. Many of us have said, "If there is anything I can do, just call me." We are sincere when we make such a comment; however, many people feel embarrassed to have to call and ask for what you offered. As I explained in an earlier chapter, my boss took the assertive approach at the time of my separation and asked me what I needed financially, so I encourage you to say, "Now tell me, what do you need? What can I do for you right now?"

Angels are always ready to lighten our load in life by helping us carry the weight of our responsibilities and problems. You can be an angel whenever you say to someone who may be feeling overworked or overwhelmed, "Let me take care of you." You may make the offer to babysit, so parents can have an evening of solitude and relaxation. Make an observation of the demands being made on another and step in, like an angel would, to shoulder some of the responsibilities for an hour, for a night, or even a weekend. I fully understand that each of us must be responsible for our own life, but every now and then it's nice to hear someone say, "I'm going to take care of you. You don't have to lift a finger."

In Windsor, New York, there's an order of Roman Catholic nuns who oversee a spiritual retreat center. I often visit the center to give my angel workshops or to participate in other activities. Recently I was speaking with Sister Elizabeth on the phone, complaining about all the hectic activity that was going on in my life and expressing my deep need for an upcoming retreat that I was planning to attend. Sister Liz said to me, "Just get yourself here, Janie, and we'll all take care of you." I felt as if her comforting words had come from heaven.

Angels never place a price tag on their service. Therefore, whatever your occupation may be, make it a practice to do just a little more than you are paid for. Always remember that an opportunity to serve is an opportunity to give and receive blessings—to progress spiritually.

The angels don't concern themselves with doing only what is required or what they are directly "paid for." Know that God is the source of your supply and all the good in your life. If you are not compensated in one way, you will be in another.

Since God is always giving to us through the angels, we might look at our lives and ask, "What can I give away today to someone?" If you don't have an abundance of money or material items to share, you can share your smile, your laughter, share your time, your energy, and your caring heart.

Angels are interested in everything we do, so in order to qualify as an earth angel you need to be interested in others. Do you rush blindly to get where you're going, or do you stop to help others along the way? I remember once when I was on vacation in England, I stopped to ask someone for directions. He was so happy to be of service and said to me, "Now do you want directions for the quickest way there or can I tell you how to take the scenic route so you'll be able to see our beautiful countryside?" I've always remembered this person's desire to share the beauty of his native land with me.

Do you say "I love you" or do you wait for others to tell you they love you first? Do you wait for love before you give it? Do you spend more time asking for help than in offering it? Maybe the help you need for yourself is waiting for you *as a result* of the service you provide to others.

When we do our holiday gift-shopping or birthday-present buying, do we buy only for those who give to us in return? Do we only swap presents? Think about someone in your life to whom you could give a gift who might not be able to reciprocate. Be an angel on a secret mission of love. Try doing it without the person knowing who it was. Now *there's* a satisfying feeling!

Be an angel and serve unselfishly. We have been so conditioned by our culture to focus on what we can get from the world instead of what we can give. Concentrate on your service and pour your heart essence into it. You will be surprised to find how good will flow back to you more easily and in many wonderful ways. Give yourself freely and abundantly to life and love life fully. It's guaranteed to get your mind off your worries, allow your needs to be fulfilled, and give you the space you need to discover the solutions the angels are offering you.

Be like the angels and experience happiness in serving. Cayce reading 3659-1 explains the blessings one receives by serving: "[Apply] self . . . towards being a means of help to someone else. And let the joy of this alone bring its own reward in peace and harmony, and in a pleasing personality."

God wants us to be aware that every second, every moment of eternity He cares for us and sends the angels to constantly remind us of His love. I recently heard a teenager reply when being lectured on why not to use drugs, "Who cares?" We need to show the people in our lives, both young and old alike, that we care about their feelings, their safety, and their health. We need to remind our youth that we care about them.

Listen to some of the comments being made in our society. It is unfortunate, but too often you hear people saying, "You can't trust anyone"; "Everyone is out for all they can get"; or "It's a me, me, me culture." If we choose to merely wait for things to change, we will have a long wait. We need to start the change within ourselves by serving God now in our own lives. Practice the messages of the angels by offering honesty, kindness, and consideration in your thoughts, words, and deeds.

Look around you for opportunities to be of service. First, look within your own family, and then at your friends, neighbors, and community. The angels are always ready to be of help to their earth siblings. Are we as equally responsive?

One way in which I encourage people to commune with the angels is by getting together with their friends and working in service as a group called an "Angel Alliance." As I shared with you in Chapter Four, I am a firm believer in the power of prayer and healing circles. Through these circles people are able to magnetize and multiply their healing energies with the energies of the angels and work together in service to God. There is an equally powerful energy formed when people get together to serve in an "Angel Alliance." By their joint human effort, as well as with the assistance of the angels working with them, their service is magnetized and multiplied.

When you have created an "Angel Alliance" with your friends, work together to come up with ideas for service. I was recently told of two people who buy $100 worth of groceries every Christmas and leave them on the porch of a needy woman in their neighborhood early in the morning. They've been doing this for fifteen years, and the woman—whom these people know socially—still has no idea who it is. Little conspiracies like that don't sound like much, but there's no better way to serve God than to serve those who live around us.

Meditate together on other ways in which your "Angel Alliance" can serve the world. For example, the homeless can now be found in nearly every community. Commune with the angels and open yourselves to receiving an angelic inspiration on what your group can do for them.

Perhaps one Saturday a month you can get together as a group and clean up a road, or visit a hospital, or remove graffiti, or stage a bake sale to raise funds for a worthy cause. Perhaps you could get together and collect blankets for the homeless and distribute them when the weather is cold. As an individual and as a group member, go within your heart and ask yourself, "What can I do to serve?" and "What can we do to serve together?" The angels will inspire you.

In what other ways can we be angels? I've adapted an old game to help us think of words that describe ways to be angelic. It's fun to do in a group. As you pass the phrases around, each player has to remember all the previous ones. You start with A and go through the alphabet to Z, assigning an angelic action to each letter. It's the ABC's of being an angel. My list begins something like this:

I WANT TO BE AN ANGEL TODAY,
SO I WILL BE ONE WHO:

Appreciates life

Blesses all things

Cooperates with all kingdoms

Delivers messages of hope

Encourages and inspires

Forgives

Generously gives to others

Heals and helps others . . .

(And so on, all the way to Z.)

Think of your own list of ways in which you can be an angel today and wrap your wings around the lives of others. It'll bring you closer to the angels and closer to accepting the truth that we are all one with God, and all have the opportunity to be ministering spirits.

In Chapter Two, I discussed the nine orders of the angelic realm as outlined by Dionysius. I would like to propose a tenth order to the angelic realm comprised of a Choir called "The Angels of Earth." I have aspired to be an angel on earth ever since I was a child. I would think about the time of my death, and in my child-like imagination, I would picture myself being greeted by the beloved Jesus, welcoming me with open arms among the angels. I would imagine Him saying to me, "Well done, my faithful servant. Your wish is now granted. You may now join the angels."

What a joy it would be to be a full-time angel and have the powers of heaven available to fulfill angelic missions. Of course, I realize that humans do not "become" angels, because we are members of a different kingdom. Yet, I believe that honorary membership is definitely possible, and that is still my aspiration.

One day I shared my heartfelt desire to be an angel with a client while I was conducting an Angelic Attunement. What was supposed to have been a session devoted to counseling for my client turned into one that brought forth a message to me. The aura of the session took on a blazing, powerful feeling of love and light which enveloped me as though I had never experienced love up until that moment. The woman, who is also practiced at meditating with the angels, felt guided to give the following message to me: "They say, 'You are already an angel.' "

It took a moment for the message to sink in, but finally I made the leap of faith and came to realize that we can all be angels. I share this important message with you because we truly are the tenth Choir of angels—the Angels of Earth. It is up to us to bring each other God's message of eternal love.

It's neither far-fetched nor childish to want to be an angel. I remember reading the story of Mary Martin who, as a little girl in Weatherford, Texas, made a wish that she could fly—not in an airplane—but like an angel through the air. Years later, Mary's wish came true when she was offered the role of Peter Pan on Broadway. The role gave her the opportunity to fly angel-style in every performance. If, like Mary Martin, you want to fly in spirit, you can do so through service. The feeling of freedom that service gives you is truly transcendent and transforming.

There's a story from the Civil War about a Confederate soldier named Sergeant Kirkland. He risked his life to crawl out onto the battlefield to the side of a wounded Union soldier who was calling for water. Once there, Sergeant Kirkland served him water from his own canteen. He placed his coat over the soldier's body to keep him warm. During the moments when he was out on the field administering as an angel, the firing miraculously would stop, but the minute he went back over the wall to get more water, the firing from both sides would resume. He was later given the name "The Angel of Marye's Heights" because the soldier had ministered to his enemy. Are we willing to do the same?

In 1854, during the Crimean War, Florence Nightingale organized one of the first hospital units. She fought many bureaucratic battles and overcame many challenges to secure necessary supplies and establish sanitary reforms that were unheard of prior to her intervention. For her work among the soldiers she was called "the angel of Balaklava." Poet George Pope Morris honored her by saying, "'Tis ever thus, when in life's storm, Hope's star to man grows dim. An angel kneels, in woman's form, And breathes a prayer for him."[6] Are we willing to overcome challenges to serve?

My mother is to me the perfect example of an earth angel. If God had put her in charge of the Garden of Eden, there would have been no fall, as she wouldn't have let Adam and Eve *near* the tree until she was finished weeding. She not only has two green thumbs but, rather, a total of ten green fingers. Everything she touches grows and everyone's life that she touches prospers just like the flowers in her guardianship.

She's always giving. You never leave her house empty-handed. If you won't stay for dinner, she'll send you out the door with a boxed dinner. She shares her food, her flowers, and most especially her love. She shares everything she has, and the most beautiful gift she shares is her smile. She is an earth angel who is always giving, a caretaker for all that God has entrusted to her hands—a husband, six children, a home, animals, and plants.

We have the power and the free will to choose to be

angels. Each and every moment of our lives we make choices. We choose whether to be happy or sad. We choose whether to be expansive or restricted, strong or weak. We choose whether or not to experience the love of the angels and to reflect that love to others by being angels ourselves.

The greatest gift that the angels give to us is love. As we know, the power of love is unequalled. It heals all things. Unconditional love knows and accepts that all life comes from God. When we want to be like the angels, we open ourselves to the experience of expressing understanding and tolerance for all people. We know that each individual who comes into our lives is doing the best according to where he or she is on the spiritual path. Just as the angels constantly express God's harmony through their service, we, too, can bring peace and order to this world of disarray and confusion by sharing our love with others, where they are.

At a time when the earth is experiencing the ravages of exploitation and new wars seem to emerge without fail, many are feeling a sense of emergency. While a lot of people feel helpless, staring into the face of issues like pollution, the disappearing ozone layer, and the vanishing of the tropical rain forests, many others are doing something dynamic in service to the earth, all over the world. You could resolve to send healing to the earth every day when you meditate, and you could participate, as I do, in the annual World Healing Meditation.

I am an avid supporter of this one-hour meditation that has taken place every year since 1986 on December 31 at 12:00 noon, Greenwich time. The World Healing Meditation was written by John Randolph Price and first appeared in his book, *The Planetary Commission*. Since 1986, millions of people have turned this into a global event. During the one-hour service, people around the world gather in spirit to visualize world peace and simultaneously send out their love and light in meditation, prayer, song, or whatever form of worship is most meaningful to them.

As part of my service to the earth, I organize groups in Maryland who participate in this annual global mind-link. Each year in November I begin sending out press releases to newspapers and television and radio stations. I run ads in community newspapers inviting the public to participate in the event on their own or attend a group meditation. Every year, from both the mayor of Baltimore and the governor of Maryland, I obtain a proclamation that December 31 is both the city's and state's World Healing Day.

I sincerely believe that when enough people around the world link their minds and hearts on the ideal of world peace, a shift in global consciousness will take place and peace will reign. Apparently, World Healing Day is continuing to grow in popularity, so that belief is slowly becoming a reality. The Quartus Foundation for Spiritual Research, Price's organization, estimates that the first year as many as 50 million people participated in the meditation, and it has grown every year since. Price himself refers to the annual World Healing Day event as a spiritual "Super Bowl" in which "the prize is peace for all people."[7] As December 31 approaches every year, I grow excited with the prospect that millions around the world will be of one mind that day. This year and every year I hope you'll make the World Healing Meditation a part of your service to the earth.

The meditation should be read aloud in unison by as many people as you can gather. It reads as follows:

World Healing Meditation[8]

In the beginning
In the beginning *God.*
In the beginning God created the heaven and the earth
And God said, Let there be light: and there was light.

Now is the time of the *new* beginning.
I am a co-creator with God, and it is a new Heaven
    that comes,
as the Good Will of God is expressed on Earth
    through me.
It is the Kingdom of Light, Love, Peace, and
    Understanding.
And I am doing my part to reveal its Reality.

I begin with me.
I am a living Soul and the Spirit of God dwells in
    me, as me.
I and the Father are one, and all that the Father has
    is mine.
In Truth, I am the Christ of God.

What is true of me is true of everyone,
for God is all and all is God.
I see only the Spirit of God in every Soul.
And to every man, woman, and child on Earth I say:
I love you, for you are me. You are my Holy Self.

I now open my heart, and let the pure essence of
    Unconditional Love pour out.
I see it as a Golden Light radiating from the center of
    my being,
and I feel its Divine Vibration in and through me, above
    and below me.

I am one with the Light.
I am filled with the Light.

I am illumined by the Light.
I am the Light of the world.

With purpose of mind, I send forth the Light.
I let the radiance go before me to join the other Lights.
I know this is happening all over the world at
    this moment.
I see the merging Lights.
There is no one Light. We are the Light of the world.

The one Light of Love, Peace, and Understanding
    is moving.
It flows across the face of the Earth,
touching and illuminating every soul in the shadow of
    the illusion.
And where there was darkness, there is now the Light
    of Reality.

And the Radiance grows, permeating, saturating every
    form of life.
There is only the vibration of one Perfect Life now.
All the kingdoms of the Earth respond,
and the Planet is alive with Light and Love.

There is total Oneness,
and in this Oneness we speak the Word.
Let the sense of separation be dissolved.
Let mankind be returned to Godkind.

Let peace come forth in every mind.
Let Love flow forth from every heart.
Let forgiveness reign in every soul.
Let understanding be the common bond.

And now from the Light of the world,
and the One Presence and Power of the Universe responds.
The activity of God is healing and harmonizing
    Planet Earth.
Omnipotence is made manifest.

I am seeing the salvation of the planet before my
    very eyes,

as all false beliefs and error patterns are dissolved.
The sense of separation is no more; the healing has
    taken place,
and the world is restored to sanity.
This is the beginning of Peace on Earth and Good Will
    toward all,
as Love flows forth from every heart,
forgiveness reigns in every soul,
and all hearts and minds are one in perfect
    understanding.
It is done. And it is so.

It is my hope that during the reading of this book you
have felt closer to the angels and to the message they bring
of God's eternal love for you. I give thanks to God for this
opportunity to introduce you to these glorious celestial
beings of light.

I've seen it happen in the lives of many whom I teach. If
you earnestly apply the principles of this book each day,
and practice the prayers and meditations, you will begin to
see how the angels play a part in your life. You will see it
in your outer life and in your inner life—in your thoughts
and in your meditations. Awareness linked with desire
will bring an anchoring into your world, one which will
benefit you in many ways throughout your life. With
intensified dedication to serving your fellow man, woman,
and child, you can actually see your world blend and
become one with the angelic realm.

As you ponder this idea of service, I'd like to offer you
this special closing reverie which I call, "Dedication to the
Light." The light of God shines through all life, and it is to
this light that I have dedicated my life in service.

Dedication to the Light

Breathe in deeply and feel the divine light expanding from within your heart.

Believe that something new will happen for you as you open yourself to the possibility of an exhilaration you haven't experienced before. Allow yourself to feel a newness within you. Though this book is coming to an end, your new experiences with the angels have given you a new beginning. This could be the beginning of your recognition that you are a part of the kingdom of the angels—a part of God. Perhaps it has deepened the awareness that you already had. Do you feel you belong in this wonderful world of infinite light and splendor? Know that you are welcomed and embraced by your celestial guardians of light.

Visualize yourself entering the doors of a magnificent temple. In front of you is a large procession of angels walking down the center aisle. You become aware that the angels are part of a beautiful dedication service. In fact, you realize that they are part of a ceremony honoring you. This is a ceremony dedicating your new awareness of the angelic realm in your life. You are coming before the heavenly host to dedicate yourself in service to the light.

See yourself walking down the aisle. As you look to the right and left of you, you may become aware of the loving faces of the angelic host who are sharing in this joyous celebration with you.

You arrive at the front of the temple and step up to the altar where you are greeted by the magnificent presence of Archangel Michael. You bow before Archangel Michael, and he raises his luminous sword upward toward heaven and proclaims, "You have chosen to dedicate yourself to the light. We, who are gathered here, serve as witnesses to your dedication and salute the light of God which pulsates within you. The light of God is now charged in your every thought, word, deed, and feeling. There is nothing in your life less than perfection. There is nothing in your life that does not radiate the light of God. Realize that whatever challenges or tests or trials may arise, they are simply opportunities to use the light of God. The light of God within you expands and unifies you with the Company of Heaven."

Now, the light of God gives you a threefold blessing. You hear the voices of the angels rejoice in unison, saying: "You are the servant. You are the serving. You are the service. Know that in all that you do—your labor, work, and service—you are the one who fulfills the mission of what you have come to accomplish. You alone are the servant for fulfilling your life. Know that with every thought, word, feeling, and action, you are the act of service. And know that the effect of your actions, whether they be physical, mental, emotional, or spiritual, will be of service to God from this point forward."

The power of the light of God is eternally victorious. Know that as you accept this power within you, you will receive unprecedented assistance from the angels in your transformation into a being of light.

At this time, visualize yourself kneeling before Archangel Michael. He gently touches your right shoulder with the tip of his sword and says, "Gratefully acknowledge in your mind and accept in your heart the ever-expanding protection of the mighty armor of God's light in your life." He gently touches your left shoulder with the tip of his sword and says, "Gratefully acknowledge in your mind and accept in your heart the filling of your consciousness with the light of God's illumination, understanding, and constancy of service."

The mighty Archangel then moves the tip of his sword to the top of your head and says, "Gratefully acknowledge in your mind and accept in your heart that the light to which you dedicate yourself is also dedicated to you. Go forth and express the light through your life in all activities balanced in God's love, wisdom, and power for all these things thou art."

Visualize yourself rising to your feet. You now stand before Archangel Michael and are becoming aware of the powerful vibration of love being sent from his heart to yours. You sense your heart open, accepting the love and radiating your love in return. Now, feel the profound joy of knowing that you are dedicated to the light and that you are finally able to shed your old illusions and put on a new reality of harmony and balance. A balance and harmony exist between your ego personality and your Higher Self. There is no longer any conflict between your ego and God's will for you. Allow yourself to remain in this beautiful exchange of love as long as you wish. When you are ready, bring your consciousness back to the room.

What is your purpose in life? Many people don't know the answer to this question. To many people, life, its direction and its scope, are little more than a blur. Even people who consider themselves to be religious move throughout their days hoping that what they believe turns out to be true, without knowing the deep, vital God-reality that underlies all consciousness, all life, and all phenomena. Where is the clarity that can dispel the confusion? Where is the proof that can erase the doubt?

The truth is that the answers to all these questions are to be found in your heart. As sure as God's name is I AM THAT I AM—the name He gave Moses from the burning bush—the I AM THAT I AM part of you burns brightly, deep within the burning bush of your heart. It's the simple truth that is perhaps too simple to be perceived by the modern mind. But it's the simple truth that is the angels' specialty. It's in finding that truth, clarity, and proof that the angels can help you the most.

I hope that in reading this book you had a wonderful experience with the angels or at least began to feel the presence of your own Guardian Angel. If you're still skeptical, I hope that you have at least allowed the possibility that God has indeed provided emissaries for us and that now, more than ever, His emissaries stand and play and work right along with us every day and every hour. But if you do believe or have actually had an angelic experience, whether from reading this book or before, it's my prayer that you will continue to "lighten up" and practice the meditations and prayers I've shared with you.

Healing, loving, and forgiveness. Sharing, attuning, and taking the dramatic leap of actually expecting blessings in your life. I hope you will allow the angels to magnify and amplify all the good you would receive and all the good you would give to others in God's name.

Let the blessings flow to you. And let them flow out to others. Seek with anticipation the many ways, both expected and especially the unexpected, in which the angels can bless your life.

They are willing and waiting to help you lift yourself from all limitation and emerge into the full expression of your true God-reality. You have the power and the free will to choose to invite them into your life—so I say, "Don't wait another minute!"

Know that the entire company of heaven stands in readiness to answer your call. And know that all you have to do is to decide, in your personal life, to shed your self-imposed limitations and, like the angels, to take your wings and FLY!

Notes

Chapter One

Believe in the Angels

1. Alex Jones, *Creative Thought Remedies* (Marina del Ray: DeVorss & Company, 1986), p. 3.
2. Flower A. Newhouse, *Rediscovering the Angels* (Escondido, Calif.: The Christward Ministry, 1950), p. 109.
3. Charles Fillmore, *The Revealing Word* (Unity, Mo.: Unity School of Christianity), p. 13.

Chapter Two

Learn About the Angels

1. *The Golden Legend of Jacobus de Voragine* (Volume II, Ryan-Ripperger translation, 1941), p. 617.
2. Manly P. Hall, *The Blessed Angels* (Los Angeles: The Philosophical Research Society, Inc., 1980), p. 28.
3. Dionysius the Areopagite, *The Mystical Theology and The Celestial Hierarchies* (Surrey, England: The Shrine of Wisdom, 1965), p. 14.

4. *Ibid.*, p. 39.

5. *Ibid.*, p. 43.

6. *Ibid.*

7. *Ibid.*, p. 46.

8. *Ibid.*, p. 18.

9. Tellis S. Papastavro, *The Gnosis and The Law* (Tucson: Balkow Printing Company, Inc., 1972), p. 63.

10. Patricia Diane Cota-Robles, *Your Time Is at Hand* (Tucson: The New Age Study of Humanity's Purpose, 1992), p. 78.

11. *Ibid.*, p. 181.

Chapter Three

Meditate with the Angels

1. Joel S. Goldsmith, *The Art of Meditation* (New York: Harper & Row, 1984), p. 6.

2. *The Secret of the Golden Flower*, trans. Richard Wilhelm. Commentary by Carl G. Jung (New York: Harcourt, Brace and World, 1962), p. 40.

Chapter Four

Pray with the Angels

1. Dr. William R. Parker and Elaine St. Johns, *Prayer Can Change Your Life* (Englewood Cliffs: Prentice-Hall, Inc., 1957), p. ix.

2. Phyllis Hobe, *The Guideposts Handbook of Prayer* (Carmel, N.Y.: Guideposts, 1982), p. 13.

3. Charles Fillmore, *The Revealing Word* (Unity, Mo.: Unity School of Christianity), pp. 10-11.

4. H.C. Moolenburgh, *A Handbook of Angels* (Essex, England: The C.W. Daniel Company Limited, 1988), p. 205.

5. Sangreal Foundation, Inc. *The Office of the Holy Tree of*

Life (Dallas: Sangreal Foundation, Inc., 1970), pp. 62-63.

Chapter Five

Share with the Angels

1. Robert Fulghum, *All I Really Need to Know I Learned in Kindergarten* (New York: Villard Books, 1989), p. 6.
2. Rev. Bruce Larson, *There's a Lot More to Health Than Not Being Sick* (Garden Grove, Calif.: The Cathedral Press, 1981), p. 43.

Chapter Six

Healing with the Angels

1. Fr. Alessio Parente, O.F.M., Cap., *Send Me Your Guardian Angel, Padre Pio* (Foggia, Italy: Editions, 1984), p. 113.
2. *Ibid.*, p. 115.
3. *Ibid.*, p. 176.
4. Flower A. Newhouse, *Rediscovering the Angels* (Escondido, Calif.: The Christward Ministry, 1950), p. 106.
5. William Bloom, *Devas, Fairies, and Angels: A Modern Approach* (Glastonbury, England: Gothic Image Publications, 1986), p. 27.
6. *Ibid.*, p. 28.
7. Robert Kent Myers, *Shaping Your Personal Vision for a New World Order* (Euclid, Ohio: RKM Enterprises, Inc., 1992), cassette tape.

Chapter Seven

Honor the Angelic Presence in All Life

1. Patricia Diane Cota-Robles, *Take Charge of Your Life* magazine (Tucson: The New Age Study of Humanity's

Purpose, September, 1990), p. 13.

2. Geoffrey Hodson, *The Angelic Hosts* (London: The Theosophical Publishing House, Ltd., 1958), p. 25.

3. Dionysius the Areopagite, *The Divine Names* (Surrey, England: The Shrine of Wisdom, 1957), p. 32.

Chapter Eight

Attune with the Angels

1. William Bloom, *Devas, Fairies, and Angels: A Modern Approach* (Glastonbury, England: Gothic Image Publications, 1986), p. 24.

2. Stuart Wilde, *The Quickening* (Taos, N.M.: White Dove International, Inc., 1988), p. 1.

3. Patricia Diane Cota-Robles, *The Next Step* (Tucson: The New Age Study of Humanity's Purpose, Inc., 1989), p. 10.

4. Herbert B. Puryear and Mark A. Thurston, *Meditation and the Mind of Mind* (Virginia Beach: A.R.E. Press, 1975), p. 11.

5. Max Heindel, *The Web of Destiny* (London: L.N. Fowler & Company, 1928), p. 124.

6. Charles Fillmore, *The Revealing Word* (Unity, Mo.: Unity School of Christianity), p. 34.

7. David Spangler, *Attunement* (Moray, Scotland: The Findhorn Foundation), p. 12.

Chapter Nine

Expect Angelic Blessings

1. Fr. Pascal P. Parente, *Beyond Space* (Rockford, Ill.: Tan Books and Publishers, Inc., 1961), p. 106.

2. Rev. J. Oatmar, Jr., and E.O. Excell, "Count Your

Blessings" (Chicago: Hope Publishing Co., 1925) as reproduced in *Hymns for Christian Service* (Chicago: Tabernacle Publishing Co., 1958), p. 78.

Chapter Ten
Be an Angel

1. Eleanor Doan, *The Speaker's Sourcebook of 4,000 Illustrations* (Grand Rapids: Zondervan Publishing House, 1960), p. 21.

2. Flower A. Newhouse, *Rediscovering the Angels* (Escondido, Calif.: Christward Ministry, 1950), p. 102.

3. Alice A. Bailey and Djwhal Khul, *Ponder on This* (New York: Lucis Publishing Company, 1971), p. 364.

4. Albert Einstein, *Out of My Later Years* (New York: Philosophical Library, Inc., 1950), p. 36.

5. John Wesley, *The Letters of the Rev. John Wesley, A.M.*, *Vol. III*, ed. by John Tolford, B.A. (London: The Epworth Press, 1931), p. 96.

6. J. Carter Swain, *Body, Soul, and Spirit* (New York: Thomas Nelson & Sons, 1957), p. 51.

7. John Randolph Price, "Commission Update: World Healing Day Five" (Boerne, Tex.: The Quartus Foundation, 1990), p. 1.

8. John Randolph Price, *The Planetary Commission* (Boerne, Tex.: The Quartus Foundation, 1984), p. 157.

Group Prayer Services

The following organizations provide ongoing prayer services for requests made by phone or mail:

Angel Power Healing Circle
c/o Angel Power Fellowship, Inc.
P.O. Box 4713
Carmel-by-the-Sea, CA 93921
(408) 624-2108
Members of the Angel Power group will pray for you every day, several times a day, for at least two weeks.

A.R.E. Prayer Services
P.O. Box 595
Virginia Beach, VA 23451-0595
(804) 428-3588
Write or phone your requests for prayer on any need. You may also join the prayer group, wherever you live, as a prayer participant by requesting to do so.

Silent Unity
Unity School of Christianity
Unity Village, MO 64065
(816) 246-5400
Write or call Unity about any kind of need, and they will pray with you. Prayer services are available 24 hours a day, 7 days a week.

For Further Reading

Bloom, William. *Devas, Fairies and Angels: A Modern Approach.* Glastonbury, England: Gothic Image Publications, 1986.

Burnham, Sophy. *A Book of Angels.* New York: Ballantine Books, 1990.

Burnham, Sophy. *Angel Letters.* New York: Ballantine Books, 1991.

Cota-Robles, Patricia Diane. *The Next Step.* Tucson: The New Age Study of Humanity's Purpose, 1989.

Cota-Robles, Patricia Diane. *Your Time Is at Hand.* Tucson: The New Age Study of Humanity's Purpose, 1992.

Dionysius the Areopagite. *The Divine Names.* Surrey, England: The Shrine of Wisdom, 1957.

Dionysius the Areopagite. *The Mystical Theology and The Celestial Hierarchies.* Surrey, England: The Shrine of Wisdom, 1965.

Godwin, Malcolm. *Angels, an Endangered Species.* New York: Simon and Schuster, 1990.

Hall, Manly P. *The Blessed Angels.* Los Angeles: The Philosophical Research Society, Inc., 1980.

Hodson, Geoffrey. *The Angelic Hosts*. London: The Theosophical Publishing House, Ltd., 1958.

Hodson, Geoffrey. *Brotherhood of Angels and of Men*. London: The Theosophical Publishing House, Ltd., 1973.

Leadbeater, C.W. *Invisible Helpers*. Adyar, India: The Theosophical Publishing House, Ltd., 1956.

MacGregor, Geddes. *Angels—Ministers of Grace*. New York: Paragon House, 1988.

Maclean, Dorothy. *To Hear the Angels Sing*. Hudson, New York: Lindisfarne Press, 1980.

Moolenburgh, H.C. *A Handbook of Angels*. Essex, England: The C.W. Daniel Company Limited, 1988.

Newhouse, Flower A. *The Kingdom of the Shining Ones*. Vista, California: The Christward Ministry, 1955.

Newhouse, Flower A. *Rediscovering the Angels*. Escondido, California: The Christward Ministry, 1950.

Parente, Fr. Alessio, O.F.M., Cap. *Send Me Your Guardian Angel, Padre Pio*. Foggia, Italy: Editions, 1984.

Parente, Fr. Pascal P. *Beyond Space*. Rockford, Illinois: Tan Books and Publishers, Inc., 1961.

Price, John Randolph. *The Planetary Commission*. Boerne, Texas: The Quartus Foundation, 1984. (The Quartus Foundation, P.O. Box 1768, Boerne, TX 78006-6768.)

Sugrue, Thomas. *There Is a River*. Virginia Beach: A.R.E. Press, 1970.

Taylor, Terry Lynn. *Guardians of Hope: The Angels' Guide to Personal Growth*. Tiburon, California: H.J. Kramer, Inc., 1992.

Taylor, Terry Lynn. *Messengers of Light*. Tiburon, California: H.J. Kramer, Inc., 1990.

What Is A.R.E.?

The Association for Research and Enlightenment, Inc. (A.R.E.®), is the international headquarters for the work of Edgar Cayce (1877-1945), who is considered the best-documented psychic of the twentieth century. Founded in 1931, the A.R.E. consists of a community of people from all walks of life and spiritual traditions, who have found meaningful and life-transformative insights from the readings of Edgar Cayce.

Although A.R.E. headquarters is located in Virginia Beach, Virginia—where visitors are always welcome—the A.R.E. community is a global network of individuals who offer conferences, educational activities, and fellowship around the world. People of every age are invited to participate in programs that focus on such topics as holistic health, dreams, reincarnation, ESP, the power of the mind, meditation, and personal spirituality.

In addition to study groups and various activities, the A.R.E. offers membership benefits and services, a bimonthly magazine, a newsletter, extracts from the Cayce readings, conferences, international tours, a massage school curriculum, an impressive volunteer network, a retreat-type camp for children and adults, and A.R.E. contacts around the world. A.R.E. also maintains an affiliation with Atlantic University, which offers a master's degree program in Transpersonal Studies.

For additional information about A.R.E. activities hosted near you, please contact:

A.R.E.
67th St. and Atlantic Ave.
P.O. Box 595
Virginia Beach, VA 23451-0595
(804) 428-3588

A.R.E. Press

A.R.E. Press is a publisher and distributor of books, audiotapes, and videos that offer guidance for a more fulfilling life. Our products are based on, or are compatible with, the concepts in the psychic readings of Edgar Cayce.

We especially seek to create products which carry forward the inspirational story of individuals who have made practical application of the Cayce legacy.

For a free catalog, please write to A.R.E. Press at the address below or call toll free 1-800-723-1112. For any other information, please call 804-428-3588, extension 220.

A.R.E. Press
Sixty-Eighth & Atlantic Avenue
P.O. Box 656
Virginia Beach, VA 23451-0656